Masters
of cinema

Stanley
Kubrick

CAHIERS DU
CINEMA

Krohn

Contents

5   **Introduction**

7   **From Photography to Cinema**
From *Fear and Desire* to *Killer's Kiss*

19 **From Hollywood to London**
From *The Killing* to *Lolita*

39 **Superstar**
From *Dr. Strangelove* to *A Clockwork Orange*

63 **Enigma**
From *Barry Lyndon* to *Eyes Wide Shut*

96 Chronology

98 Filmography

100 Selected Bibliography

Sue Lyon in *Lolita* (1962).

Introduction

Stanley Kubrick's cinema accompanied my era and my generation. I can remember the date of my sister's marriage because I sneaked out of the rehearsal dinner wearing my tux to see *Lolita*, knowing that, dressed as I was, I wouldn't be questioned about my age at the ticket window. I took a train from New Haven to New York to see *Dr. Strangelove*, and when I returned, I joined a campus anti-nuke organization — for all of a week.

By the time *A Clockwork Orange* opened I was living in New York. As my friends and I lined up to see it, Katharine Hepburn came storming out of the previous show, her face so red that you couldn't see the freckles. Wife and hearth were on the line in that film, and in *Straw Dogs*. The ideological aims of classical cinema had become obvious to a child.

As exaggerated as this will sound, these early Kubrick films, especially *2001*, sent shock waves all over the world. But after *A Clockwork Orange*, Kubrick withdrew from the public eye, and going to see his new films ceased to be a collective or even a necessary act — it took me years to get around to seeing *Barry Lyndon*, and by the time I caught up with *Eyes Wide Shut*, it was showing in a shabby theatre in Los Angeles, where the projectionist turned off the projector and closed the curtain during the final credits.

If Kubrick had still been alive, that projectionist would have heard from him. 'Exhibitors in Midwestern cities would be startled', John Baxter writes in his biography, 'by a low, toneless Bronx murmur announcing, "This is Stanley Kubrick. Your number two projector is out of alignment. An engineer will be there this afternoon. Meanwhile, don't use it."' The cinematic prophet of my generation never really went away. By connecting him to his era in this book, I hope to show that he is as present today as ever.

Stanley Kubrick in the 1960s.

From Photography to Cinema

From *Fear and Desire* to *Killer's Kiss*

Stanley Kubrick during the shooting of *Dr. Strangelove* (1964).

Right: Kubrick's first photograph published in *Look* magazine in April 1945: a news vendor reacting to the death of Franklin D. Roosevelt.

Following pages: 'Prizefighter', Kubrick's photo-essay on a middleweight boxer named Walter Cartier (1949).

The Bronx

Stanley Kubrick was born on 26 July 1928 (between world wars), to the children of Austrian immigrants (from the region of Galicia), and grew up in a section of the Bronx that was a magnet for New York City's Jewish middle class. His family was Jewish but not religious. His father Jack taught him to play chess when he was twelve, and for his thirteenth birthday gave him his first still camera.

Of all the fairies gathered round the cradle (two great wars and the Shoah, America and Europe, Judaism, photography, chess), the ring-leader may well have been chess. Like many great filmmakers, Kubrick was an eccentric, and chess masters are often eccentrics too. Those seeking to elucidate the Kubrick mystery should read the portrait of a grandmaster in *The Defense* by Vladimir Nabokov, whose most famous book Kubrick filmed in 1962.

Chess is an abstract representation of war, the principal subject of Kubrick's films, which can be seen in retrospect as having encompassed the major conflicts in which the United States was involved during the twentieth century: World War II (*Fear and Desire*, 1953 — which also alludes to the Korean War, in progress when the film was made), World War I (*Paths of Glory*, 1957), the Cold War (*Dr. Strangelove*, 1964) and the Vietnam War (*Full Metal Jacket*, 1987), as well as an unplanned excursion to a slave revolt in Ancient Rome (*Spartacus*, 1960), a cancelled magnum opus about Napoleon, and a film whose first act is set against the last years of the Seven Years War (*Barry Lyndon*, 1975).

Kubrick was a terrible student — he told a classmate whose homework he was in the habit of copying that school just didn't interest him. Curiously, although he got an 'F' in high-school English, he did read a book he came across in his father's waiting-room when he was fourteen: Humphrey Cobb's World War I novel *Paths of Glory*, which he eventually filmed.

From *Look* Magazine to *Fear and Desire*

Photography was a way of getting around his shyness. He became the photographer for the Taft High School magazine, where he made friends who would later become collaborators. He also played drums in a jazz group. At seventeen, he sold his first photograph to *Look* magazine, a 'candid' shot of an old news vendor looking dejected, framed by front pages announcing the death of FDR, and was hired by *Look* as an apprentice photographer.

He spent five years at *Look*, during which he married his high-school girlfriend Toba Metz and moved into a small Greenwich Village apartment. At around this time Kubrick, already a cinephile, started devouring foreign films.

In 1949 he and Alex Singer, a friend from the school magazine, made a nine-minute documentary inspired by 'Prizefighter', Kubrick's photo-essay on a middleweight boxer named Walter Cartier. *Day of the Fight* (1951) was sold for a miniscule profit to RKO, which commissioned Kubrick to make a second short about an itinerant priest in a Piper Cub aircraft. By then he had already quit his *Look* job to concentrate on filmmaking.

The consent decree obliging Hollywood studios to divest themselves of their cinemas had made it possible for films to be made and exhibited outside the studio system, and Kubrick was one of the early pioneers. He and Taft friend Howard Sackler wrote an ambitious film about four soldiers trap-ped behind enemy lines in a war that looks a lot like World War II, despite mixing and matching of war-surplus uniforms to make the conflict look 'generic'. (Sam Fuller's independently produced Korean War film *The Steel Helmet* had been a surprise hit on Times Square in 1950.) Financed by Kubrick's parents and a rich uncle, *Fear and Desire* was filmed on location with a cast of unknowns in California's San Gabriel Mountains.

Kubrick, who shot the film with a camera that he learned how to load when he rented it, was virtually the whole crew. His production costs tripled when he set about creating a soundtrack for the film, which had been shot without sound because, ironically, he had thought that would save money. So, post-production had to wait while he directed a short documentary for a mariner's union, and second unit sequences for a television mini-series about Lincoln scripted by James Agee, to raise the needed funds. What is never said when that story is told is that the sound edit of all the parts in *Fear and Desire* is very good, including a striking overlapping montage of the men's thoughts that accompanies a montage of hiking footage.

Kubrick persuaded art-house pioneer Joseph Burstyn to take on the film — a first for Burstyn, whose most famous exploit was winning a court case against the Catholic League of Decency over Roberto Rossellini's *The Miracle*. Years after that first release, Kubrick withdrew *Fear and Desire* from

circulation[1] because he considered it an embar-
rassment, but he didn't always feel that way. In
1952 he wrote to Burstyn: 'Its structure: allegorical. Its conception: poetic. A drama of "man" lost
in a hostile world — deprived of material and spir-
itual foundations ...' The letter goes on to equate
film with poetry, and poetry with ambiguous allegory — not a bad description of the kind of films
Kubrick would make.

Fear and Desire is full of stylistic tributes to
art-house filmmakers — Kurosawa, Welles, Ophuls,
Buñuel, Eisenstein, De Santis (Bitter Rice) — but
Kubrick is already fusing European ideas with a
Hollywood genre as filmmakers like Scorsese and
Coppola would do in the 1960s. Descriptions of
Kubrick as an anti-Hollywood filmmaker over-
look the fact that his oeuvre was always aimed
at Hollywood, although he was never interested

in playing by the studios' rules. The subversion of
Hollywood began with his films' content and grad-
ually affected their form. Only in late films like Full
Metal Jacket does he set out to 'explode the conven-
tions of narrative cinema' in a way that mirrored
his favourite theme, already present in his first film:
the struggle between reason and chaos.

In Fear and Desire the authority of the lieutenant, the squad's rationalistic leader, is under-
mined for us immediately by the snidely superior
way he talks, and later by external factors. At the
end of the film, one soldier is insane and another is
dead, while the two survivors have become affect-
less after encountering older versions of themselves
(cf. astronaut Dave Bowman at the end of 2001)
and killing them.

The metaphor underlying Fear and Desire
is the one with which Gilles Deleuze defines all

of Kubrick's cinema: a brain that malfunctions.[2] Sometimes the 'brain' that breaks down is an individual; sometimes it's a group engaged in a collective enterprise (war, nuclear deterrence, space exploration) that gets tripped up by accident or error, or by a group member who derails the enterprise when he goes crazy. Although Deleuze probably hadn't seen it, his observations about Kubrick apply quite well to *Fear and Desire*, where the four men in the squad, we're told, 'inhabit no country but the mind'.

Repetitions 1 and 2: *Killer's Kiss*

Kubrick's next project, a film noir written with Howard Sackler, was made in New York City for a somewhat larger budget than his first. Mindful of how expensive all the dialogue in *Fear and Desire* had been, Kubrick described *Killer's Kiss* (1955) to *The New York Times* as 'a tragic, contemporary story that depends more on visual effects than on dialogue'. Although he finally decided to go for an un-tragic ending, United Artists bought *Killer's Kiss* half-heartedly and distributed it in the same spirit. The film received good notices for its cinematography and a flashback-within-a-flashback to a ballet performed for the camera by Kubrick's second wife, Ruth Sobotka.

Killer's Kiss completes a trilogy of sorts in which Kubrick portrayed the same subject — boxing — as

Opposite page: Virginia Leith and Paul Mazursky in *Fear and Desire* (1953).

Right: Virginia Leith and Steve Coit in *Fear and Desire* (1953).

a photographer, as a documentarian and as a fiction filmmaker. Filmmaker Alex Cox tells Jan Harlan[3] in his documentary *Stanley Kubrick: A Life in Pictures* that the appearance of the soundtrack album for *2001* in a record store in *A Clockwork Orange* (1971) signifies that, beginning with *2001*, Kubrick's only influence would be himself. In fact, Cox is describing a creative method that Kubrick employed from the beginning of his career, which is so important in his oeuvre that it could be said to be its generating principle: repetition. While repetitions from film to film are typical of the work of cinematic auteurs, the sheer number of them in Kubrick's oeuvre gives it a dense, closed, systematic feeling.

The way 'Prizefighter' generated *Day of the Fight* is an example. Kubrick's first short film turns his photo-essay, which was accompanied by terse, neutral captions, into a critique of the sport (*Repetition 1*). The opening shots show a fan buying his ticket. What does he want to see? Violence, blood. He doesn't think about the men who fight, the narrator tells us, or their reason for fighting: money. Boxing is a job — one that doesn't pay very well.

The short film is mostly about the time before a fight, during which the boxer takes a long look at his face in the mirror as if saying goodbye to it. Before that we see him take communion 'in case something goes wrong tonight'. The fight is shown in all its brutality from the point of view of spectators who are screaming for blood. Cartier is white; his opponent is black. We're already in Peter Ustinov's gladiator school in *Spartacus*.

Cartier is accompanied in the photo-essay by his twin brother and manager, Vince. This bizarre detail becomes more important in the short, as does the apartment they are sharing before the fight, which becomes a haven to hide from the empty and vaguely sinister streets of the city outside. Unlike the essay, the film doesn't show Cartier's girlfriend Betty — this haven is for men only.

The Cartier brothers' gender uniformity is mirrored by the persistent oddity of their twinhood— when we first see them they are sharing the same bed, and later we are told that each blow that lands on Walter that night will be felt by Vincent, as if they were telepathically linked. Kubrick is already portraying the all-male professional group, a theme

Killer's Kiss

Davy (Jamie Smith) has made an appointment to meet Gloria (Irene Kane) at the dance hall, where her boss, Rapallo, is supposed to give her her last pay cheque. Davy's manager, Albert (Jerry Jarrett), is also coming there to pay Davy for his last fight. Afterwards the couple will catch the train to Seattle.

But two drunken conventioneers accost Davy and take his scarf, obliging him to pursue them. Rapallo threatens Gloria when she comes to his office. She leaves without her cheque and waits for Davy at the door to the dance hall. Albert arrives and stands next to her. They have never seen each other, but both are waiting for Davy, whom Rapallo's henchman have been ordered to kill. The first henchman tells Gloria to go back to the office, where she will now receive her pay cheque with a bonus. When she's gone, the henchmen take Albert away, having mistaken him for Davy, and kill him in a back alley.

The sequence has been condensed here by one big omission – Kubrick intercuts between Davy and Gloria throughout as he did systematically at the beginning of the film, as they put on their work clothes, go to their places of business and do their jobs (boxing, taxi dancing). Focusing just on the events in the doorway brings out the chess metaphor in the sequence, where Davy's queen is taken first and then his rook. Kubrick later said that the 'Watch Your Step' sign just happened to be in the location he chose, but we can assume he chose it in the first place because of the chessboard-like linoleum on the landings.

There are two henchmen, two conventioneers and two men waiting, one of whom is mistaken for the other – the first of many scapegoats in Kubrick's œuvre, which presumes this kind of interchangeability between characters. The twinhood of the boxer and his manager evident in *Day of the Fight*, absent from Davy's story until now, has returned and is spreading like a virus through the body of the film.

Opposite page: 'Kid Rodriguez' and Jamie Smith in *Killer's Kiss* (1955).

Right: Irene Kane and Jamie Smith in *Killer's Kiss* (1955).

Irene Kane in *Killer's Kiss* (1955).

he inherited from Hollywood war and action films, in a way that makes it appear strange, even uncanny. The disquieting sensation of uncanniness will play an increasingly important role in his cinema. Here it is evoked by the theme of the double, which Sigmund Freud links to the phenomena of twins and telepathy, and to all forms of repetition (including Nietzsche's 'eternal recurrence'), in his essay 'The Uncanny', which Kubrick read years later when he was preparing to film *The Shining* (1980).

The fight in *Killer's Kiss* repeats the situation of waiting from the Cartier documentary and a few visual ideas such as a poster stuck on a lamp-post, which is now part of a montage that prophetically includes a shot of feet walking over the same poster in the rain. As Davy, the hero, prepares for the fight he's going to lose, he stares at the mirror and experimentally pushes in his nose the way Cartier did. Then Kubrick shows him peering through a goldfish bowl, a deforming shot that makes him look like a battered pugilist.

The image also underlines the fact that Davy, unlike Cartier, has no companion but the goldfish in his one-room apartment. His solitude will drive him into an involvement with the woman who lives across the courtyard: Gloria, a dime-a-dance girl who looks a lot like Grace Kelly. (Hitchcock's *Rear Window* was released the previous year.)

The repetition of the scenography of *Rear Window* in *Killer's Kiss* is an example of another form of repetition by which we will see Kubrick's oeuvre take shape and grow, despite Cox's assertion that he eventually freed himself from it: the influence of other filmmakers (*Repetition 2*). Kubrick creates his first static shot-sequence in *Killer's Kiss*, using the

view of Davy's apartment from Gloria's as a pretext — Davy's eyeball peers through the curtains at the police searching his own apartment across the way, played without a cut, like the little courtyard dramas in *Rear Window*.

When this type of shot becomes a signature stylistic device, the staring eyeball will be inscribed in the off-space, its exterior position underlined by the filmmaker's refusal to cut to a reverse angle, and non-cinematic scenographies — theatre and painting — will be used to frame the staring images. Like Orson Welles, Kubrick transformed classical models to make a new kind of cinema where shot-sequences do not serve the aims of realism — a formal innovation that would take on greater importance in his next film.

Opposite page: Jamie Smith in *Killer's Kiss* (1955).

Right: James Stewart and Grace Kelly in Alfred Hitchcock's *Rear Window* (1954).

Below: Jamie Smith and Irene Kane in *Killer's Kiss* (1955).

From Hollywood to London

From *The Killing* to *Lolita*

Vince Edwards and Marie Windsor
in *The Killing* (1956).

The master of ceremonies

The next phase of Kubrick's career was shaped by his partnership with a well-to-do young producer he had met through Alex Singer, James B. Harris. *The Killing* (1956) was based on a novel by Lionel White, *Clean Break*, and was scripted by pulp fiction genius Jim Thompson. *Killer's Kiss* had been financed by a family friend; *The Killing* was produced by United Artists, once the partners secured a commitment from a fading star, Sterling Hayden. Filmed in Los Angeles, it was Kubrick's first professional production, with a good cast and a great cameraman, Lucien Ballard, who didn't enjoy working for a director who was a gifted cameraman in his own right.

The Killing portrays a heist masterminded by a professional criminal that goes badly wrong. Kubrick and Thompson follow the novel closely except for the factor that makes the well-oiled machine self-destruct. In the book, all the problems are caused by George, the pathetic character played by Elisha Cook, Jr, who blabs about the plan to his scheming wife. As in the film, this leads to a shoot-out that leaves George the last man standing. But it is only in the book that he subsequently kills the planner of the heist, Johnny Clay, impelled by the delusion that Clay is running off with George's wife and the loot.

Although they use George to eliminate most of the gang, Kubrick and Thompson add two more representatives of chance in the film: a friendly black guard who offers the triggerman a 'lucky horseshoe' (his hand falls next to it when he is killed) and a silly rich woman whose little dog causes a series of accidents that send the stolen money flying off in the backwash from the plane's propellers, delivering Clay to the plainclothes cops assigned to watch the airport.

The numerous static shot-sequences in *The Killing* are smaller versions of the bigger 'pieces of time', each featuring a different character, that compose the film's non-linear narrative. The whole idea of embedding shot-sequences in larger pieces of time comes from *Citizen Kane* (1941), a film that posed a real threat to Kubrick's quest for originality. By way of contrast, Max Ophuls' influence,[4] proudly acknowledged, did not threaten Kubrick. Sobbed over by Nelson Riddle's strings, James Mason delivers as flawless an Ophuls performance in *Lolita* (1962) as he had in Ophuls' *Caught* (1948); the spacecraft in *2001* (1968) waltz to the strains of *The Blue Danube*; and the camera becomes Alex diving out a window

in *A Clockwork Orange* (1971) as it does when the model attempts suicide at the end of *Le Plaisir* (1952).

The example of Ophuls helped shape the narrative archetype of the malfunctioning brain, which finds its first full expression here. Two of Ophuls' late films feature a character who seems to stand for the director: Anton Walbrook's master of ceremonies in *La Ronde* (1950) and Peter Ustinov's ringmaster in *Lola Montès* (1955). But Ophuls expert William Karl Guérin[5] has taught us to be suspicious of the master of ceremonies. He is a Mephistopheles whose pleasure at reducing the other characters to elements in a narrative structure 'illustrates a sinister conception of man' — a conception that has often been attributed to Kubrick. In fact, Ophuls had it in for this figure, and so did Kubrick, as we can see in his treatment of Johnny Clay in *The Killing*.

Clay, an ex-con who spent four years planning a 'perfect' racetrack robbery in his jail cell,

Opposite page: Sterling Hayden in *The Killing* (1956).

Right, top: Peter Ustinov and Martine Carol in Max Ophuls' *Lola Montès* (1955).

Right, bottom: Anton Wallbrook and Simone Signoret in Max Ophuls' *La Ronde* (1950).

is the master of ceremonies, the mind that holds together all the pieces of the complex plan: all the characters in the film. He is defeated by external factors, as if the cosmos itself is rebuking his pretensions to omniscience, but also by his own foibles. One character's observation at the beginning of the novel could be the basis for Kubrick's portrayal of his protagonist: 'The man must have some sort of anxiety complex.'

Clay himself malfunctions in the film: running '15 minutes late' because of traffic, he tries to open the door of the rented bungalow where the money has been dropped, only to realize that it's the identical bungalow next door. 'Sorry. I made a mistake', he says. And his rigid insistence that he must leave on schedule when the airline won't let him carry on the bag full of money destroys him in the end. Clay's representative on the soundtrack is the film's documentary-style narrator, who seems to be speaking Clay's thoughts in the third person — a portentous off-screen Voice that Kubrick subtly parodies. For one thing, the Voice is a little *too* obsessive, indulging in pointless precision about time, like the announcement that begins the film: 'At exactly 3.45 on that Saturday afternoon, Marvin Unger was the only person in the crowd …'

On the other hand, Kubrick expert Mario Falsetto points out that the narrator himself, who is so obsessed with precision, also makes mistakes. For example, he announces: 'It was exactly 7.00 a.m. when [Johnny] got to the airport', which flatly contradicts his earlier statement that 'at 7.00 a.m. that morning Johnny began what might be the last day of his life'.[6] The Voice seems to have forgotten a whole scene that has occurred between the time Johnny got up and the time he went to the airport, one added by Kubrick and Thompson, where Marvin makes a clumsily disguised declaration of love to Johnny.

Ironically, when chance delivers Clay into the hands of a racetrack guard who spots him leaving after the robbery, he is saved by Marvin, who got drunk after being spurned and has shown up at the racetrack contrary to Clay's orders. Here, an irrational element that the Voice literally seems not to have noticed – Marvin's love for Johnny – comes to Clay's rescue in a sequence that plays without any narration, as if the Voice still does not see Marvin's actions. But variations on Marvin's irrationality, such as the desperate love of George's wife for a good-looking young gangster, ultimately foil Clay's plans, bringing the narrative that is a reflection of his obsessive mental processes to a catastrophic conclusion.

On visual style considered as a game of chess

The next Harris–Kubrick film, *Paths of Glory*, filmed in Germany and based on the anti-war novel Kubrick read as a teenager, could not have been made without actor–producer Kirk Douglas, who expected that it 'wouldn't make a dime' but felt that the story of three French soldiers executed as scapegoats for a blunder of the High Command during World War I had to be told. As a sop to Douglas's female fans, the star is not wearing a shirt in his first scene.

Like *Dr. Strangelove* and *Full Metal Jacket*, *Paths of Glory* is about an army subverted by an aberrant event: a general who orders his men to attack an impregnable hill. Banned in France as an insult to the army, the film had to be made in Munich and could not be shown in France and Belgium (where veterans' groups had it pulled from cinemas) or in Spain, Switzerland and Israel, which had reciprocal censorship agreements with France.

Kubrick told Michel Ciment that he preferred adaptations because a book makes such a strong impression on first reading.[7] 'That first impression is the most precious thing you've got', he adds; 'the yardstick for any judgement that you have as you get deeper and deeper into the work.' This may explain something that makes even admirers of *Paths of Glory* uneasy: the artless naivety of the film's *cri de coeur* against injustice. If what Kubrick says is true, the film is a faithful transposition of the impression the book made on him when he first read it, when he was fourteen years old.

Paths of Glory is a painful story, which the director wished to modify as he had when he gave

Above: Marie Windsor and Sterling Hayden in *The Killing* (1956).

Opposite page: Stanley Kubrick with Vince Edwards and Marie Windsor on the set of *The Killing* (1956).

Killer's Kiss a happy ending. Douglas refused to let him insert a last-minute stay of execution, but he found another way to end on a hopeful note. A scene was added where the comrades of the murdered men are moved to tears by a captured German girl singing a song in her native language. (She was played by Christiane Harlan, who became Kubrick's third wife, and with whom he would raise three daughters.) But even that 'happy ending' is subverted by the film's style.

Although devices like the static shot-sequences deployed in *The Killing* hark back to Welles, Kubrick told Alexander Walker it was Ophuls who was the inspiration for his visual style. Here is the famous quote: 'I did very, very much like Max Ophuls' work. I loved his extravagant camera moves which seemed to go on and on forever in labyrinthine sets … I don't think Ophuls ever received the critical appreciation he deserved for films like *Le Plaisir*, *The Earrings of Madame de …* and *La Ronde*. When I went to Munich in 1957 to make *Paths of Glory* at the Geiselgasteig

Studios, I found the last sad remnants of a great filmmaker — the dilapidated, cracked and peeling sets that Ophuls had used on what would prove to be his last film, *Lola Montès*.'[8]

Kubrick dedicated the first day of shooting on *Paths of Glory* to Ophuls, who had just died, but the image of waltzing dignitaries in the film, reminiscent of so many Ophuls scenes, is filmed as a lateral tracking shot that is also an example of Kubrick quoting Kubrick, since it recalls the lateral tracking shots of the shuffling clients at the dance hall in *Killer's Kiss* and the bored women who have been paid to dance with them.

In his review of *The Killing*, Jean-Luc Godard correctly described the camera movements as cold copies' of Ophuls' style.[9] Kubrick's most frequent camera moves are a lateral tracking shot that recalls the movement of the eye reading a page, and a simple dolly-out or dolly-in, accomplished with slow zooms in *Barry Lyndon*. Such shots decompose Ophuls' tracking shots, which

sinuously combine movement along both axes, into geometric abstractions.

    The shots in the trenches in *Paths of Glory* that dolly back from an officer who is advancing or walking forwards, to show, from his point of view, the cowering men lined up on either side of the trench, suggest another geometric form because Kubrick shot them with a Wellesian wide-angle lens.[10] Because of the slight deformation imposed by that lens, our eye perceives these shots as arcs of a huge circle — a rhyme to the little circle the camera traces while it is following General Mireau and his superior in a grandiose office (filmed on the day Kubrick dedicated to Ophuls) as the superior tells Mireau that if he doesn't order the suicide attack, someone else will.

    These circles — geometric abstractions of Ophuls' idea of the 'round of life' — symbolize the closed system of military authority in which even the noble Colonel Dax (Kirk Douglas) is complicit because he sees no alternative to it. The same argument that assuages the ambitious Mireau's conscience induces Dax to lead the attack. Circular movements are the signal that one of the characters has been caught in the trap of 'playing the game', as Dax is when he starts walking briskly to an off-screen drum in the last shot, preparing to lead his demoralized company back into battle.

    More than the occasional shots of figures standing on black and white tiles (like the trial scene in *Paths of Glory*), the varied uses Kubrick finds for these few simple movements recall the game of chess, where a few schematic moves generate an infinite number of gambits. The recurrence of these simple geometrical forms in film after film reinforces the impression of an oeuvre built out of repetitions.

Kubrick in Hollywood

Paths of Glory put Kubrick on the map. Its success led to two loan-outs: he spent months developing *One-Eyed Jacks* (1961) with Marlon Brando, and when it became apparent that Brando wanted to direct the film himself, Kubrick was hired by Kirk Douglas to direct a film Douglas was producing and starring in about a gladiators' revolt in Ancient Rome, after the first director, Anthony Mann, had been fired.

Hired on a weekend, Kubrick walked onto the set on the Monday and took charge, proceeding to tame a lion's den of English actors — Laughton, Ustinov, Olivier — whose competitive intrigues mirrored their roles in the film. *Spartacus* (1960) became the top-grossing picture of the year. Filmed on sound stages and the Universal backlot, with the slick look of all Universal films of the period, *Spartacus* is a subversive story clothed in the artifice of Hollywood's last golden age … with a few adjustments.

For example, Kubrick's habit of playing scenes in one static shot, from a bit of a distance. The fact that the studio sets and painted backdrops of *Spartacus* were being filmed this way outraged the screenwriter, Dalton Trumbo, who seems to be channelling his former employer, Louis B. Mayer, in his memo to Douglas after seeing the rough cut: 'I am saddened by the fact that we do the scene … almost as a master scene, instead of going for the marvellous details of reaction', he says of the interlude when the

Above and right: Kirk Douglas in
Paths of Glory (1957).

Stanley Kubrick on the set of *Paths of Glory* (1957).

Opposite page: Stanley Kubrick
with Tony Curtis during
the shooting of *Spartacus* (1960).

Above: Kirk Douglas and
Woody Strode on the set of
Spartacus (1960).

Following pages, left:
Kirk Douglas in *Spartacus* (1960).

Following pages, right: Stanley
Kubrick with Kirk Douglas
on the set of *Spartacus* (1960).

former slave, played by Tony Curtis, recites a poem for the rebels. 'Why could we not have gone from face to face in this scene while the poetry is read, so we can get to *know* these slave people?' While Douglas did eventually make Kubrick shoot some insipid scenes of life in the freed slaves' camp to be intercut with the sequence, no reaction shots were added to Kubrick's 'master scene'.

The practice of inventing through repetition continued. As rewritten by Peter Ustinov and Kubrick, the scene where two gladiators, played by Kirk Douglas and Woody Strode, fight to the death while bored Romans gossip about politics, paying no attention to the bloody spectacle, repeats the scene in *Killer's Kiss* where Gloria's boss seduces her while they are watching Davy getting pulped on TV.

And once annexed, *Spartacus* became part of Kubrick's oeuvre, with the power to generate shots and scenes in the films that followed it. 29

In *A Clockwork Orange*, the scene when Alex is unable to rape the topless blonde bombshell offering herself to him in front of a bunch of government big shots and scientists — a situation that is joyfully reversed in the film's last shot — comes from the book, but also harks back to Spartacus refusing to make love to the slave girl who has been offered to him in his cell because he knows his owner and his trainer are spying on them.

Repetitions 3 and 4: *Lolita*

While Kubrick was struggling with his monumental task, he and Harris acquired *Lolita*, Vladimir Nabokov's scandalous bestseller about a European professor, Humbert Humbert, who marries a widow in order to possess her twelve-year-old daughter Lolita, only to lose her to a pervert more cunning than himself. Nabokov was hired to write the screenplay, but Kubrick completely rewrote it, retaining only a few scraps of Nabokov's contribution. To play Lolita, a talent search turned up Sue Lyon, a talented fourteen-year-old who looked mature enough to avoid criminal penalties for the filmmakers.

An English company produced the film with money from the Eady Fund, and to enhance the project's English identity, Kubrick cast a second English actor, Peter Sellers, to play opposite his choice for Humbert, James Mason. *Lolita* was made in England, where Kubrick and his family decided to settle and where all his films would be made after this. Afflicted by fear of flying, even though he had a pilot's licence, he would eventually choose a self-imposed exile, but he was still crossing the Atlantic at this point and was able to personally direct the footage illustrating Humbert and Lolita's car odyssey across America — a job that would be done by second units after he stopped flying altogether.

Kubrick said in a piece he wrote for *Sight & Sound* while he was preparing *Lolita*: 'When the director is not his own author, I think it is his duty to be one hundred per cent faithful to the author's meaning'. It is remarkable that such an original artist, after his first two features, would choose to film only adaptations. His approach resembles that of Luis Buñuel, a filmmaker he admired, whose adaptations of works such as *Nazarín*, *Tristana* and *The Diary of a Chambermaid* disclose a vein of anarchist thought in each that is congenial to his temperament. One thing Kubrick's film has

Sue Lyon and James Mason in *Lolita* (1962).

By portraying American mores, notably adolescence, as if seen from the moon, and alternating sentimental sequences with farcical ones where Humbert plays the straight man to a parade of oversexed grotesques, like Tom Cruise in *Eyes Wide Shut*, Kubrick remains faithful to the social and sexual meanings of Nabokov's story. Today, when the purists' outrage over Sue Lyon's breasts has died down, *Lolita* has not aged at all. An act of cinematic imagination comparable to the one that gave us the novel has given us Hum and Lo for the ages, miraculously alive (*Repetition 3*).

The ending of the film, which repeats the opening shots, enables us to glimpse a form of repetition that became a much-publicized obsession in Kubrick's later years: the mountain of takes he ordered of every individual shot in a film like *The Shining* (*Repetition 4*). *Lolita* only appears to begin and end with the same shot of Humbert walking into Quilty's cluttered mansion — different takes were used. In the first take, Quilty is in the background asleep in an armchair, hidden under a sheet with a bottle balanced on his head, but when the film circles back after a four-year flashback to show Humbert's entrance again, there is no bottle — and perhaps no Quilty under the sheet — 'as if Humbert has walked into a parallel nightmare where his righteous revenge may never be satisfied' (writes Richard Corliss).[11]

Actually, the bottle perched on Quilty's head is present in the shot, but only at the beginning — by the time the camera finishes its trajectory, it has disappeared. Did it fall off accidentally while the camera was dollying, or did someone sneak in and remove it — the director, perhaps? Internet legend has it that we can see Kubrick for a few frames during the dissolve from the exterior to the interior of Quilty's mansion at the beginning of the film, ducking out of the shot as Mason enters.

This symbolic vanishing was one way to exorcise the influence of Welles, which is so blatant with respect to visual style (wide-angle lenses, deep focus, high-contrast photography, shot-sequences) and narrative construction in Kubrick's black-and-white films. Kubrick chose Ophuls as his artistic father over Welles, who is in front of the camera in most of his films, whereas Ophuls, who also started as a stage actor, is not — certainly not in the guise of the master of ceremonies. Instead, those elegant

in common with Buñuel is that — to paraphrase Jean-Pierre Oudart's defence of *A Clockwork Orange* (a film that Buñuel loved) — you don't have to have a degree in semiotics to understand its critique of America in the 1950s.

'How did they ever make a movie of *Lolita*?', asked the film's ads, establishing the direction that criticism has followed ever since by making the issue of censorship the centre of all discussion. Kubrick, of course, does not show Humbert copulating with Lolita, although there is no doubt that that is what is going on. Instead, as in some of Buñuel's Mexican films (e.g. *Susana, demonio y carne*), sexuality is a diffuse presence from which there is no escape. Kubrick keeps sex in the forefront of the spectator's mind with displays of sexual aggression by women who crave Humbert and non-stop dialogue double entendres, so compulsive as to be a bit sinister: 'Is this a plot to expose me?', Humbert seems to wonder at moments when he literally doesn't know what to say to some leering remark. 'Is everyone in on it?'

camera movements imply the presence of an invisible master whose onscreen absence is never filled in, not even by a Hitchcockian cameo.

As it happens, in Welles's most Ophulsian film, *The Magnificent Ambersons* (1942), he is absent from the image but present on the soundtrack, where Kubrick would also turn up occasionally in his own films: as a voice on the radio in *The Shining*, and as a voice on a walkie-talkie in *Full Metal Jacket*. Peter Tonguette, the critic who told me about those fleeting aural cameos, also points out a mysterious apparition in Kubrick's last film: seated next to the hero's table in the nightclub where he has gone to talk to Nick Nightingale is Kubrick himself, or his double.

In Jean-Claude Biette's valedictory study of Kubrick and *Eyes Wide Shut* (1999), he makes the director's disappearance the foundation of his cinema: 'All his life or almost, Kubrick invented and made films from which he excluded himself … To the heights from which Welles — his model — never stopped descending … Kubrick never stopped ascending to create oversized, closed-off worlds for stupid, grimacing gods to wander about in.'[12] But Kubrick still had one more film to make before the shadow of Welles would vanish — at least in appearance — from his cinema.

34   James Mason, Sue Lyon and
Shelley Winters in *Lolita* (1962).

'Words and Movies', by Stanley Kubrick

The perfect novel from which to make a movie is, I think, not the novel of action but, on the contrary, the novel which is mainly concerned with the inner life of its characters. It will give the adaptor an absolute compass bearing, as it were, on what a character is thinking or feeling at any given moment of the story. And from this he can invent action which will be an objective correlative of the book's psychological content, will accurately dramatize this in an implicit, off-the-nose way without resorting to having the actors deliver literal statements of meaning … People have asked me how it is possible to make a film out of *Lolita* when so much of the quality of the book depends on Nabokov's prose style. But to take the prose style as any more than just a part of a great book is simply misunderstanding just what a great book is. Of course, the quality of the writing is one of the elements that make a novel great. But this quality is a result of the quality of the writer's obsession with his subject, with a theme and a concept and a view of life and an understanding of character. Style is what an artist uses to fascinate the beholder in order to convey to him his feelings and emotions and thoughts. These are what have to be dramatized, not the style. The dramatizing has to find a style of its own, as it will do if it really grasps the content. And in doing this it will bring out another side of that structure which has gone into the novel. It may or may not be as good as the novel; sometimes it may in certain ways be even better … You might wonder, as a result of this, whether directing was anything more or less than a continuation of the writing. I think that is precisely what directing should be … When the director is not his own author, I think it is his duty to be one hundred per cent faithful to the author's meaning and to sacrifice none of it for the sake of climax or effect. This seems a fairly obvious notion, yet how many plays and films have you seen where the experience was exciting and arresting but when it was over you felt there was less there than met the eye? And this is usually due to artificial stimulation of the senses by techniques which disregard the inner design of the play. It is here that we see the cult of the director at its worst. On the other hand, I don't want to imply rigidity. Nothing in making movies gives a greater sense of elation than participation in a process of allowing the work to grow, through vital collaboration between script, director and actors, as it goes along. Any art form properly practised involves a to and fro between conception and execution, the original intention being constantly modified as one tries to give it objective realization. In painting a picture this goes on between the artist and his canvas; in making a movie it goes on between people.

This is an extract from an article published in *Sight & Sound*, 30 (1960–1).

Opposite page and right: Sue Lyon and James Mason in *Lolita* (1962).

Superstar

From Dr. Strangelove to A Clockwork Orange

Stanley Kubrick on the set of
2001: A Space Odyssey (1968).

Following pages: Slim Pickens in
Dr. Strangelove (1964).

Apocalypse now

While *Lolita* was becoming a hit, Harris – Kubrick Productions bought a novel about the threat of nuclear Armageddon, which the Cuban Missile Crisis had almost brought on: *Two Hours to Doom* would be based on *Red Alert*, a deadly serious Cold War thriller written by Peter George, *nom de plume* of Peter Bryant, a retired officer of the Royal Air Force.

Before the start of production, Kubrick and Harris terminated their partnership so that Harris could pursue his own directing career, and with Harris's departure, Seven Arts dropped out of *Two Hours to Doom*. They were replaced by Columbia Pictures, who insisted on having Peter Sellers play multiple roles in the film – something he had already done in Jack Arnold's Cold War satire *The Mouse That Roared* (1959), which featured an infernal device called 'the Q-Bomb'. By the time Kubrick announced the casting of Sellers to *The New York Times*, he had hired Terry Southern, a leading exponent of 'black comedy' whom Sellers admired, to rewrite the script for what was now called *Dr. Strangelove or: How I Learned to Stop Worrying and Love the Bomb*.

Kubrick nonetheless continued to stay true to the meaning of the novel he was adapting without imitating its style: 'The dramatizing has to find a style of its own, as it will do if it really grasps the content. And in doing this it will bring out another side of that structure which has gone into the novel.'[13] Already deep into preparations for making a realistic thriller, he realized that the structure of George's story – with its tripartite montage structure showing the parallel actions of characters unable to communicate with one another – was equally appropriate to a farce, which could be even more effective at conveying the meanings inherent in it.

In a series of rewrite sessions with Southern – fuelled by industrial quantities of marijuana – even as the sets were being constructed, General Quinlen, the book's villain, became General Jack D. Ripper, who believes that the fluoridated water supply (seen by the lunatic Right of that era as a communist plot) has made him impotent. With no change in their plot functions, the characters were allocated new names and personalities based on the varieties of human sexuality. General Steele, who wants to annihilate the Russians to prevent retaliation, became the macho idiot Buck Turgidson (= male deer, son with a turgid penis), and the liberal President Merkin Muffley (merkin = pubic wig, muff = pudendum) became a homosexual: a ribald joke about the unwavering complicity of

the American Right and Left in the prosecution of the Cold War.

As with *Lolita*, the precedent for this fusion of sex and global politics (epitomized by the famous credit sequence showing a bomber being refuelled in mid-air while a love ballad plays on the soundtrack) could be certain Buñuel films from this period — for example, *La fièvre monte à El Pao* (*Fever Mounts at El Pao*, 1959), about a power struggle on a Caribbean island shaped like a woman's high-heeled shoe.

Kubrick told Alexander Walker[14] that, paradoxically, his eleventh-hour decision to turn the film into a comedy made it more realistic, whereas films like *On the Beach* (1959) and *Fail-Safe* (1964) in a misguided attempt at 'seriousness', excluded trivial details and behaviour that would be hilariously incongruous in the context of the approaching end of the world. He might have added that General

Ripper's madness was a more realistic motivation in 1962 than the rational calculations of General Quinlen in the novel, which was published in 1958. In that post-Sputnik era there had been actual discussions in military circles of a nuclear first strike after Russia successfully tested intercontinental ballistic missiles that would shift the balance of power when fully deployed.

Before Southern came on board, a script had been written for a thriller based closely on the book, and some sequences from it — especially on board the B-52 — appear to have been filmed with little or no change. Hence, as Michel Chion observes, 'the profound originality of *Strangelove*, which comes from the contrast between the buffoonery of many elements ... and the rigour of the scenario.'[15]

Made in England on sound stages and on futuristic locations, *Dr. Strangelove* (1964) was a meteor. Kubrick had fused documentary realism and grotesque comedy to portray the American military-political establishment as fools and madmen, putting on the screen for the first time the kind of satire made popular by *Mad* magazine. He now became, as much as any rock star, a hero to the Vietnam generation, who would be waiting to embrace an even more daring experiment when he unveiled it four years later.

An uncanny ascent

This time, the writing of the film, which was made under wraps in England, proceeded in tandem with the mammoth task of inventing the near future and making it look real. *2001: A Space Odyssey* (1968) was inspired by a short story Kubrick's collaborator, Arthur C. Clarke, had written about an alien artefact found on the moon. Made for showing in Cinerama, the film had no hero, portraying instead the evolution of the human race from ape

Peter Sellers

Extreme acting styles are important to Kubrick's evolving aesthetic, in which the encounter with Peter Sellers played a pivotal role. Not with respect to technique: Kubrick became known for shooting lots of takes, and Sellers was the kind of improvisational actor whose first takes needed to be captured by multiple cameras. But their collaboration on *Lolita* and *Dr. Strangelove* confirmed Kubrick's suspicion that the guts of a character might be discovered on the set. Sellers also gave Kubrick his first opportunity to display his sense of humour, which turned out to be more British than American. Kubrick's script for *Lolita* was funny, but it is the opening scene where Humbert kills Clare Quilty (Sellers) – one line in the script – that lifted the film to the heights of 'The Goon Show', the radio series with Spike Milligan and Harry Secombe where Sellers first became known. Trying to stave off death, Quilty runs through his repertory of accents, remembering all the identities he has assumed in his past.

Whatever plans Kubrick may have had to make a serious film of Peter George's novel *Red Alert* were scotched when he accepted Columbia Picture's suggestion that he have Sellers play multiple roles, as he had in Jack Arnold's sleeper hit, *The Mouse That Roared* (1959). After *Dr. Strangelove* became Kubrick's first blockbuster, an interviewer suggested to Vladimir Nabokov that Sellers should have played Humbert Humbert. *Lolita*'s creator responded: 'That would have been a wonderful idea.'

Peter Sellers (above),
George C. Scott (below)
and Slim Pickens (opposite page)
in *Dr. Strangelove* (1964).

Following pages: Peter Bull and
Peter Sellers in *Dr. Strangelove*
(1964).

to superman, guided by a mysterious extra-terrestrial intelligence.

Preview audiences found *2001* boring and incomprehensible, but the shape of the story resembled the after-life journey described in 'The Tibetan Book of the Dead', which Timothy Leary had reprinted as a guide for LSD users. Young audiences embraced the film, sold by Metro-Goldwyn-Mayer as 'The Ultimate Trip'. The success of *2001* set Hollywood on a new path: a cinema of special effects in which the only stars were the kind that twinkle in the distant reaches of outer space.

Kubrick's oeuvre is divided into two periods, before and after *2001*. Besides the introduction of colour — still discreet in this film, where the blackness of space and the whiteness of the spaceships predominate — a less visible demarcation line is traced by his ongoing struggle to overcome the influence of Welles. After a first period in which every image designated him as Welles's successor, nothing Kubrick did after *2001* resembles anything by Welles, because this is when Kubrick began making films that are like no films that had ever been seen, including his own.

Citizen Kane and *2001: A Space Odyssey* are films about influence. What made Charles Foster Kane the man he was? If we can figure out what his last words meant, we'll know. What made Man what he is? Follow the monolith and we'll find out. 'Rosebud', critics never tire of telling us, is a solution that solves nothing.[16] Can we say the same thing of Kubrick's jet-black sled without an inscription? Or have the answers given by both films been overlooked because they provoke anxiety — the anxiety of influence, which is their subject? The root of the word 'influence' is 'influenza', a sickness that was once believed to come from the stars and planets, whose alignment seems to have something to do with the action of the monoliths in *2001*.

Paradoxically, *2001* is the film where Kubrick drew the most radical conclusions from his love of Welles — it doesn't look like *Citizen Kane*, but the blocks of time used to tell the story of *Kane* inspired its form. Taking the shape of the Pindaric ode or one of its romantic descendants, with their sudden reversals between stanzas, the film designates its real subject — which is Time, not Space — in the gaps between three blocks of time whose only connection is that each contains its own monolith, its own

Above:
2001: A Space Odyssey (1968).

Opposite page: Keir Dullea in
2001: A Space Odyssey (1968).

Rosebud. Within each block, movements of imaginative contraction — the apes' daily life, boring trips to the Moon and Jupiter, a whole life played out in an eighteenth-century-style hotel room with a shining floor — are followed by movements of euphoric expansion, when the film breaks free of its narrative chains: the waltz of the spaceships, the Stargate, the birth of the Star Child.

The death of *2001*'s master of ceremonies, HAL the computer, is the signal for the beginning of the film's last movement, when the story all but evaporates in a series of non-representational images that finally coalesce back into narrative coherence in the 'hotel' where the aliens have lodged Bowman after his trip through the Stargate. It in no way detracts from Kubrick's achievement to note that he was able to overcome his anxiety about the influence of Welles, the great story-teller, by radicalizing his identification with Ophuls, who took narrative cinema in the direction of a cinema of pure forms, closer to music.

What Welles invented that makes him such a formidable predecessor was not a particular modern style or form, but the structure of modernity in cinema, what the psychic defence Harold Bloom, the American theorist of the anxiety of influence, calls 'transumption', which makes works like these possible. In the wars of creation, transumption overcomes the anxiety of influence and achieves imaginative priority (what we euphemistically call 'originality') by identifying with the precursor's precursor.

But this defence can also be expressed in a film's form — for example, the identification of

Music

Opposite page: Keir Dullea in
2001: A Space Odyssey (1968).

Above:
2001: A Space Odyssey (1968).

Gerald Fried, a graduate of the Juilliard School of Music who had been hired to score Kubrick's first short, also scored his first four features. His music for *Fear and Desire* includes a wonderful interlude with a hurdy-gurdy theme for the scene where a soldier tries to entertain a female captive with a clownish imitation of a general. Fried arranged Kubrick's first 'twisted standard': a sinister version of '*La Marseillaise*' for the credits of *Paths of Glory*. Later, British composer Laurie Johnson would use an orchestral version of '*When Johnny Comes Marching Home*' for the scenes in *Dr. Strangelove*'s B-52.

Many accounts have been published of how the classical score for *2001* was created. The likeliest explanation: Kubrick's brother-in-law, Jan Harlan, was a music expert, and when Kubrick decided to junk the score written by Alex North, he went to him for suggestions. 'I need a piece of music that rises up and comes crashing down', Harlan recalls him saying. 'Short and self-contained.' The opening fanfare of Richard Strauss's tone poem *Also sprach Zarathustra* fitted the bill.

Kubrick's next three scores used classics re-orchestrated by Leonard Rosenman (*Barry Lyndon*) and Wendy (Walter) Carlos, whose compositions were combined with synthesized versions of Beethoven, Rossini and Purcell for *A Clockwork Orange*. The choices, such as Rossini's *The Thieving Magpie* before the home-invasion sequence in *A Clockwork Orange*, demonstrate a connoisseur's wit. The most effective Kubrick score is the one attributed to Carlos for *The Shining*. With nothing to guide them but a copy of the book, Carlos and her partner Rachel Elkind guessed wrong, but finally Kubrick used their music and pieces by Bartók, Penderecki and Ligeti to create his own mix. He screened *Eraserhead* (1977) for his collaborators, presumably because he wanted to imitate the subtle 'ambiances' that David Lynch and sound designer Alan Splet had devised, adding another layer of anxiety to what is virtually a wall-to-wall soundtrack for 'the ultimate horror film'.

Kubrick was an innovator in the ironic use of pop music in film. It was the producer's brother who wrote '*Lolita Ya-Ya*', the mocking vocal that became the heroine's leitmotif in that film. '*Try a Little Tenderness*' and the World War II ditty '*We'll Meet Again*' make their comments at the beginning and end of *Dr. Strangelove*, 1920s dance tunes haunt the Overlook in *The Shining*, and the first inkling Beethoven-lover Alex de Large has that his par-

ents have taken a boarder while he was in prison are the unwelcome strains of '*I'm Going to Marry a Lighthouse Keeper*' filling his former home.

The period pop selections in *Full Metal Jacket* – from the country tune '*Goodbye Sweetheart, Hello Vietnam*' to the insanity of The Trashmen's '*Surfin' Bird*' – are especially brilliant. A rap remix of R. Lee Ermey's boot-camp diatribes didn't make it into the film, but became the number two single in England in 1987.

Under the name 'Abigail Mead', Kubrick's daughter Vivian composed the underscore for *Full Metal Jacket*, with the 'rusty gate' sound used during the sniper hunt, and for *Eyes Wide Shut*, Kubrick hired avant-garde composer Jocelyn Pook. Classical compositions by Liszt, Shostakovich and György Ligeti round out the score of his last film. For their third 'collaboration', Kubrick chose a piece Ligeti composed in communist Hungary with no expectation of ever hearing it performed. When he wrote the motif consisting of one insistently repeated note on the piano, Ligeti told Harlan: 'Every note was a knife directed at Stalin's heart.'

cinema in *A Clockwork Orange* and *Barry Lyndon* with arts that preceded it — theatre and painting — and its symbols. The nth repetition in human culture of the ancient myth of the mortal turned into a constellation after a great exploit, the Star Child audaciously presents itself as prior to all myths because it is the creation of beings that were present before the invention of culture, even before the invention of Man.

One of the oddities in criticism of *2001* is the way it fails to accurately describe the object on the screen. *2001* is an eerie film, built on the uncanny repetition of the three monoliths that appear on Earth, on the Moon and orbiting Jupiter, where astronaut Dave Bowman encounters the final one at the end of his voyage. Adding to the uncanniness of the monoliths is that of space itself (Is that a moon-taxi or a head with glowing eyes? Are we in space or at the bottom of a black ocean? Is the *Discovery* a spaceship or a skeletal, deep-sea-dwelling fish?) and of that strange hotel room on the other side of the universe.

For Kubrick's Sublime is indistinguishable from the Uncanny — a modern offshoot of the 'pleasant fear' cultivated by the eighteenth century that replaced the natural Sublime (mountains, oceans, storms) in literature around the time the Gothic novel became popular. Like Franz Kafka, he substitutes the Uncanny for traditional aesthetic modes, and like Kafka, he is an instinctive Gnostic.

Above: Heather Downham in
2001: A Space Odyssey (1968).

Opposite page:
Stanley Kubrick on the set of
A Clockwork Orange (1971).

Following pages:
Malcolm McDowell in
A Clockwork Orange (1971).

Leaning at first on the analogous tenets of existentialism (see *Fear and Desire*), Gnosticism[17] plays an increasingly important role in Kubrick's films, culminating in *2001*, where the universe is a deceptive labyrinth through which Man, in the person of Bowman, must find his way to achieve oneness with the Alien God who stands outside of material creation and against it. Intuitions of that higher reality can be had in experiences of the Sublime and the Uncanny — ambivalent sensations a Gnostic would interpret as expressions of the mind's anxiety at encountering its own infinity, which is embodied in *2001* by Pascal's 'infinite spaces', represented here for the first time in a major work of art.

Certainly, the space sirens of *2001* have a bit in common with *The Shining*'s ghosts, who promise Jack Torrance a better future, then turn him into a caveman and a block of ice. How many murders — beginning with the first ape killed — has it taken to produce the Star Child? That final image is breathtaking, but Kubrick's portrayal of humanity as the end-product of manipulations by a vastly superior external force — no more flattering, really, than the idea that a man's destiny might be shaped by the loss of a toy — leaves a strange impression once the chords of Richard Strauss's *Also sprach Zarathustra* have died away.

Repetition 5: *A Clockwork Orange*

Kubrick's Sixties climaxed with an adaptation of Anthony Burgess's novel about a dystopian future where youth gangs run amok, *A Clockwork Orange* (1971). Taking nine months to shoot using a copy of the novel as a script, it was made on London locations, transformed into a future where the Pop Art

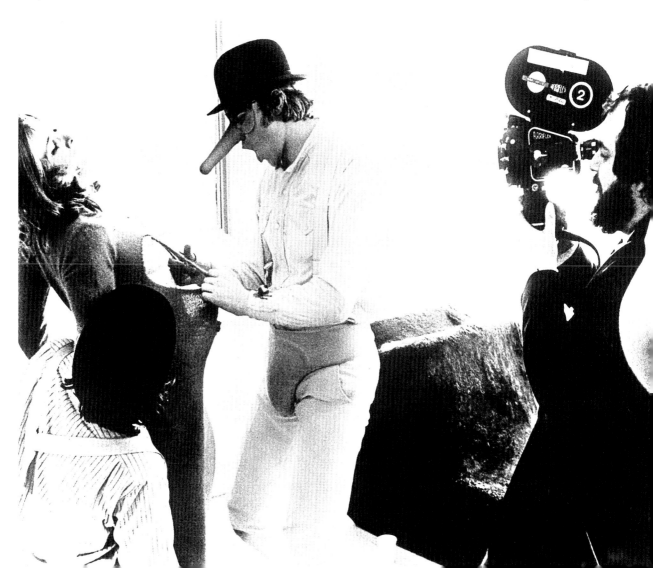

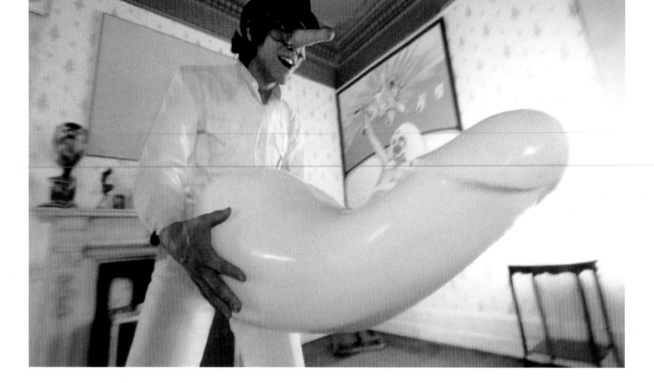

creations that supplied a backdrop for the Sixties have become mass-produced furniture and fashions. To see the film as a satire on youth culture, however, would be to drastically misunderstand the audience response that made it an international success. *A Clockwork Orange* exemplified the dark side of the Sixties — The Stones, not The Beatles — and it is still the most exhilarating cinematic expression of the period's rebellious spirit.

The film opens with a slow dolly-back from a close-up of the hero, Alex, played by Malcolm McDowell with a combination of brio and truthfulness that recalls James Cagney in *The Public Enemy* (1931) and *The Roaring Twenties* (1939). To the accompaniment of Henry Purcell's *Music for the Funeral of Queen Mary*, re-orchestrated for the Moog synthesizer by one of its creators, Walter Carlos, the camera starts on Alex's unblinking leer, then pulls back to reveal his 'droogs' ('friends' in Nadsat, the argot Burgess invented for his hoodlums to speak) and the subterranean décor of the Karova Milkbar, where plastic figures of subjugated women expose themselves, serve as tables and dispense drugs from their breasts, which incite those who drink to acts of rape and 'ultra-violence'.

Noting that this remarkable condensation of all the film's meanings into one shot was devised and filmed near the end of production, Alexander Walker writes: 'The deadly cold eyes of Alex … hold the lens inflexibly as the camera begins retreating like a courtier who fears to turn tail till the lord and master he serves is out of sight. The tableau opens up in apprehension of him and his attendant spirits … Statuary, symmetry, the sense of satanic majesty: there is a flavour of a perverse Versailles … *A Clockwork Orange* often has the look of a fantastic masque, a modern *Comus* …'[18]

Walker's references to court masques and other allegorical devices native to England, Kubrick's new home, are perfectly appropriate to this faithful adaptation of a novel by the author of a novel about Shakespeare. The masque was a courtly art form that combined poetry, music, dance, costume, décor and even special effects in a ritualistic multimedia performance addressed to all the senses. Comus was the Greek god of revels, anarchy and nocturnal trysts, usually depicted as a young man about to pass out from having too much to drink.

'Its structure: allegorical. Its conception: poetic.' That is how Kubrick described *Fear and Desire* in 1953, adding: 'It will, probably, mean many different things to different people, and it ought to …' This early statement of aesthetic principles points to the allegorical nature of Kubrick's art while stressing something that he often said in interviews: he really did prefer not to talk about the meaning of his films because he wanted them to be open to multiple interpretations. Kubrick confided to Walker that he enjoyed finding details in other directors' films that he couldn't be sure they had put there consciously — an argument against explaining enigmatic details of precisely the kind that characterize *A Clockwork Orange*.

One source of these enigmas is the first level of repetition in Kubrick's oeuvre — that between films. For example, HAL-like IMDb.com informs me that 'CRM-114', the security device that prevents the world from communicating with the B-52 'Leper Colony' as it rockets towards Russia in *Dr. Strangelove*, lurks in the name of the drug used to condition Alex against sex and violence in *A Clockwork Orange* ('Serum 114') — a point made at the time by Walker, who may have had it from the horse's mouth — and in the room number of the morgue Bill Harford visits in *Eyes Wide Shut* ('Corridor C, Room 114').

Enigmatic details are also generated by internal repetitions (*Repetition 5*). All the events in Alex's initial night on the town are repeated in the film's second half, this time with Alex the victim of those he victimized before. But these internal repetitions are no longer isolated enigmatic details. They have coalesced into a form: the uncanny narrative.

Lolita is an uncanny narrative only by virtue of its content, because it is shaped by the veiled machinations of Quilty, or of a cruel god who surely must resemble him. So is *Dr. Strangelove*, where everything conspires against the heroes'

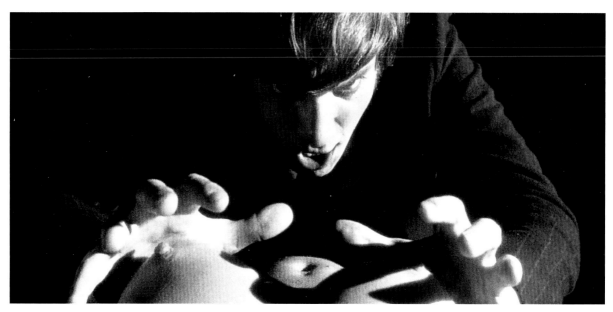

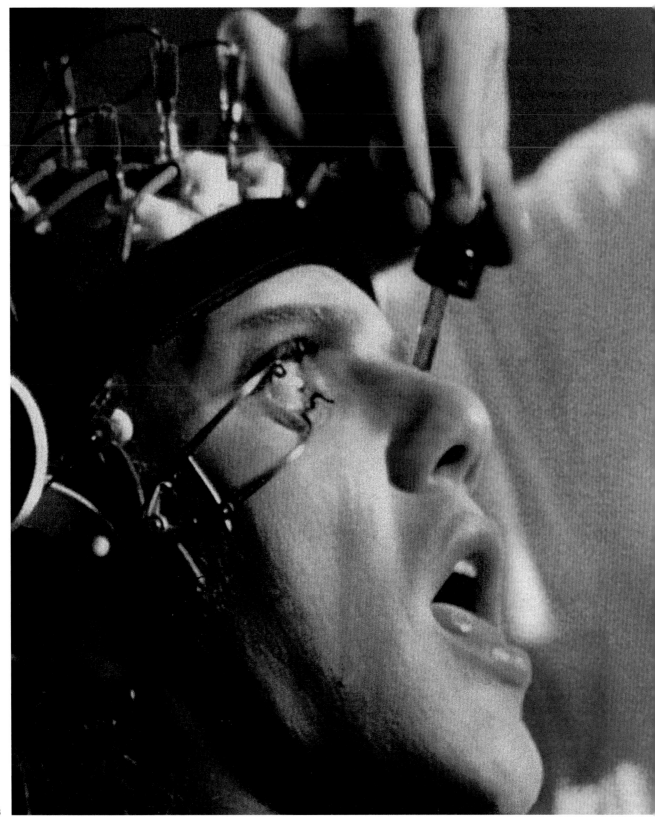

attempts to stave off the Apocalypse. Paranoia, the 1960s showed, can be political: 'In eras like this,' Jean-Pierre Oudart wrote of *A Clockwork Orange*, 'judicial scenarios become for some, and even for many … the cinema of an Other who does not mean them well, *the cinema of a cruel god*.'[19]

But in the symmetrical narrative of *A Clockwork Orange*, uncanny repetition (Kubrick called it 'magical coincidence') is deployed as an aesthetic that affects every element in the film. For Freud, the Uncanny is 'something which is familiar and old-established in the mind and which has become alienated from it through a process of repression'. This certainly applies to the repetitions in the second part of *A Clockwork Orange*, after Alex's instincts (sexual, aggressive, aesthetic) have been repressed and all the actions he joyfully performed in the first part of the film come back in inverted form to haunt him.

Who or what is Alex? One obvious answer would be the id, locked in struggle with the super-ego (the aptly named Interior Minister). As a Freudian allegory, *A Clockwork Orange* shows how man's instincts are channelled into approved forms of satisfaction through the painful detour of the Oedipus complex and the reality principle (Serum 114).

Burgess's novel champions man's God-given free will, using Alex as an extreme case to make the argument, but in the film Alex does not really have free will. His actions are performed under the influence of Milk Plus, of Serum 114 and of a society where the rich (on the Right and the Left) manipulate and despise 'the common people' (as the writer calls them), who can only acquire the goods they are programmed to want, including the drugs they are addicted to, through crime. Even Alex's 'cure' — which Kubrick makes a return of sexuality, and not of violence, as it is in the book — results from reprogramming by the Interior Minister.

In the novel, Alex truly does have free will — at least in the British edition, where the final chapter shows Alex, after his power of choice has been re-stored, reluctantly growing older and wiser, making plans to settle down and raise a family, and writing a novel with the title of the manuscript whose pages he scattered when he overturned Mr Alexander's writing desk: *A Clockwork Orange*. But Kubrick stuck to the impression left on him by the U.S. version he read when Terry Southern gave it to him during the filming of *Dr. Strangelove*, which lacked the final chapter. As Burgess notes in his introduction to the expanded 1986 American edition: 'The American or Kubrickian *Orange* is a fable; the British or world one is a novel.'

Because he is the hero of a fable, played by an actor bursting with larger-than-life vitality, Kubrick's Alex really is that uncanny figure of Cockney slang: a 'clockwork orange'. Freud begins his essay on the Uncanny by quoting Otto Jentsch, a previous writer on the subject: 'In telling a story, one of the most successful devices for creating uncanny effects is to leave the reader in uncertainty whether a particular figure is a human being or an automaton.' Uncanniness can be political, too. The German word that becomes 'the Uncanny' in English, becomes in French 'l'inquietant etrangeté' ('disquieting strangeness'), a cognate of the Brechtian term '*Verfremdungseffekt*', translated by Maurice Blanchot as '*l'effet d'etrangeté*' ('the effect of strangeness'), usually translated in English as 'distancing effect'. Brecht's *Mann ist Mann* is, after all, about a recruit being programmed by the army, a subject Kubrick would tackle head-on in *Full Metal Jacket*.

In his 1986 introduction, Burgess also notes unhappily that in Kubrick's film 'a vindication of free will has become an exaltation of the urge to sin'. To which Kubrick might reply that the instrument for seducing the spectator into seeing the world as Alex sees it was invented by Burgess himself: the Joycean language that Alex uses to tell his story. His verbal seduction draws us into identification with him, even as the images display him repeatedly — in wide-angled static shots that tend to remain on screen longer than they usually would — as a performer on a stage: perhaps the inner stage of his own mind, with whatever drug he is controlled by at the moment creating the *mise-en-scène*, whether it be Milk Plus during the first act or Serum 114 throughout his long comeuppance, during which, as Mario Falsetto observes, the style of the film changes to reflect his changed perceptions.[20]

Opposite page: Malcolm McDowell in *A Clockwork Orange* (1971).

Following pages: *A Clockwork Orange* (1971).

Enigma

From *Barry Lyndon* to *Eyes Wide Shut*

Stanley Kubrick on the set of
The Shining (1980).

Serving the text

Metro-Goldwyn-Mayer, which was about to be taken over by a speculator who planned to sell off its assets, was in no position to produce the next Kubrick film, an epic about Napoleon, and Warner Bros. also backed away from the projected costs. So Kubrick recycled his research into a period picture for Warner Bros. based on William Makepeace Thackeray's *The Memoirs of Barry Lyndon*, about the rise and fall of an Irish adventurer, played by America's number one box-office star, Ryan O'Neal. Shot almost entirely on location from a script composed of blank pages, *Barry Lyndon* (1975) took 300 days to film, and the budget had sextupled by the time Kubrick was done. It was a disaster everywhere but in France.

The *Memoirs of Barry Lyndon* is a picaresque novel inspired by the works of Henry Fielding (*Tom Jones*), whom Thackeray revered. One sometimes reads that Kubrick had no sense of humour, an odd statement in view of the fact that all his films contain some comedy, even *2001. Barry Lyndon* begins with a static shot-sequence in which two men, at a great distance from the camera, prepare to fight a duel while the narrator tells us that the hero's father intended to make a career in the law and would have excelled at it — 'Bang!' One of the men

falls — if he had not been killed in a duel. The timing is comic; the image, ravishingly beautiful: an old winding stone wall with black silhouetted trees on either side of it links the verdure of the foreground to the background where tiny figures square off under dark clouds. An unsympathetic critic might claim that the beauty of the landscape smothers the gag, but the truth is that we see and admire the landscape before the gag, a banana peel for the beauty of the image.

Nor is *Barry Lyndon* a particularly slow film, although the characters' movements are slow and the dialogue often filled with pauses. Barry's courtship of the Countess of Lyndon, spanning five years in the book, is dispatched as efficiently as his father, in a shot of O'Neal slowly approaching Marisa Berenson on a moonlit terrace, taking her hand and kissing her. This combination of slow staging and telescoped action constantly situates key events on the edge of comedy, even when Schubert is playing on the soundtrack.

The situation in *Barry Lyndon* is the reverse of *Dr. Strangelove*, where nightmare comedy was added to achieve the aims of Peter George's book by other means. *Barry Lyndon* treats a comic novel in the manner of an Ophuls film like *The Earrings of Madame de* … (1953). The awesome beauty of the Irish and English countryside supplies a melancholy frame for foolish behaviour, at the same time locating the characters' actions on the far horizons of memory, where they already existed for Thackeray.

By their stasis and formality, the film's tableaux vivants, expanded for our inspection by slow zooms back from some detail in the canvas, undercut their own realism. An example of excessive realism leading to a result that is anything but realistic are the scenes filmed by candlelight, a first in film history. In the candle-lit interiors, make-up, costumes and golden light fill the past with gilded figures who are always about to turn into waxworks or automata, like Lloyd the ghostly bartender in *The Shining*. Even in scenes filmed in natural daylight, background figures tend to hold their poses as if they were in a painting, like the card players who freeze when Bullingdon appears to challenge Barry to a duel.

Made at the height of the late 1970s fashion for historical films, *Barry Lyndon* is one of the few examples of the trend that does not make the 'effect of strangeness' a drug for the imagination of spectators who are only too happy to identify for a couple of hours with doomed figures from some aristocratic yesteryear. Here is Brecht on the effect of strangeness, in this case translated as 'distanciation': 'The aim of the distanciation effect is to extract from the process being represented the fundamental social *Gestus* that will make it appear strange. By social *Gestus* we mean the expression through gestures and facial expressions of social relations existing between men at a particular time in history.'[21]

A great deal of moralizing scholarly commentary is scraped away in Kubrick's portrayal of Thackeray's all-too-human hero. He ages Barry, who in the book is a fifteen-year-old 'Lolito' infatuated with his twenty-three-year-old cousin Nora, but retains his innocence, his bravery and his honesty, which he must have believed in when he discovered the novel and read it for the first time — otherwise, how could he have got O'Neal to embody these traits so movingly? The death of Barry's beloved child, a minor incident in the book, becomes the cause of his breakdown and the collapse of his marriage, like the death of Rhett and Scarlett's child

Reminiscence, by Bernard Williams

He said to me the week before shooting, 'Which is the most difficult scene to shoot in this movie?' I said, 'Well, the tracking shot of the British marching on the French.' He said, 'OK, we start that on Monday.' I said, 'But it's going to rain for a week.' He goes, 'OK. We'll shoot in the rain.' I said, 'OK, fine.' He said, 'Let's have a meeting the day before shooting.' So I said, 'OK.' [At the meeting] he says, 'So, the guys are marching in line, right? And I'm tracking 800 feet across this field. How do we keep all their footsteps in the same tempo?' I said, 'Well, they're from the army, Stanley.' He says, 'No, no, no – they've got to walk in unison. What have you done about that?'

I'm sitting there going [gesture of bafflement] … 'Well, Bernie,' he said, 'you need 5,000 feet of green rope. You put green rope every three feet and then they don't have to look down. They can just feel it as they walk and they'll all be in unison.' I said, 'OK. Well, we'll get the rope.' This was a Sunday. The only thing open in Ireland on Sunday is a pub and a church. Then he says, 'What are those things they put on top of pianos?' I said, 'A metronome.' He said, 'Well, let's build a big one. And we'll put it on a rostrum and we'll get a composer over from England.

And it goes tick, tick, and they go tick, tick, tick … They're all walking together.'
So I said, 'OK, fine. Is that it, Stanley?' He goes, 'What are you going to do when it rains?' And I said, 'Well, we've got big tents …' He said, 'We're not lining this up for three hours in the rain and then they rush off to the tents. What's that thing Clint Eastwood used to wear in his Westerns?' I said, 'A poncho.' He says, 'Get 500 of those for tomorrow. And get some film bags, too – one for their head and two for their feet. You'll need rubber bands for their feet. They put this over their head to protect the wigs and they wear the poncho and

you get them some sandwiches and a flask of coffee.'
I said, 'Where does this all go?' He says, 'In a bag.' I say, 'But it's not "period".' He said, 'It is today. Make up 500 bags by tomorrow and put all that stuff in it.' And that's how we went about every day – an innovation every day.

This is an extract from a conversation between Bernard Williams, line producer of *A Clockwork Orange* and *Barry Lyndon*, and Ryan O'Neal, Leon Vitali and Randy Haberkamp of the Academy of Motion Picture Arts and Sciences, after a screening of *Barry Lyndon*, 21 August 2006.

Opposite page:
Ryan O'Neal and Marisa Berenson in *Barry Lyndon* (1975).

Right: Ryan O'Neal and Leon Vitali in *Barry Lyndon* (1975).

Following pages: Stanley Kubrick with the camera crew (Doug Milsome and John Alcott) and Ryan O'Neal on the set of *Barry Lyndon* (1975).

(also in a riding accident) in *Gone With the Wind*. Kubrick was certainly not trying to make a flop.

Barry Lyndon and *A Clockwork Orange* are companion pieces because of their picaresque narratives, but *Barry Lyndon* — following Burgess's distinction — is a novel, not a fable; and Barry, despite all the talk of how he is shaped by the societies he moves through, is a character with free will, as Kubrick is at some pains to show in the most important episode he added to Thackeray's story. Although Leon Vitali says that Lord Bullingdon, Barry's jealous stepson, had only one dialogue scene when he was cast to play him — the character gets eight pages in the book[22] — the director expanded the role, making Bullingdon Barry's nemesis, and invented

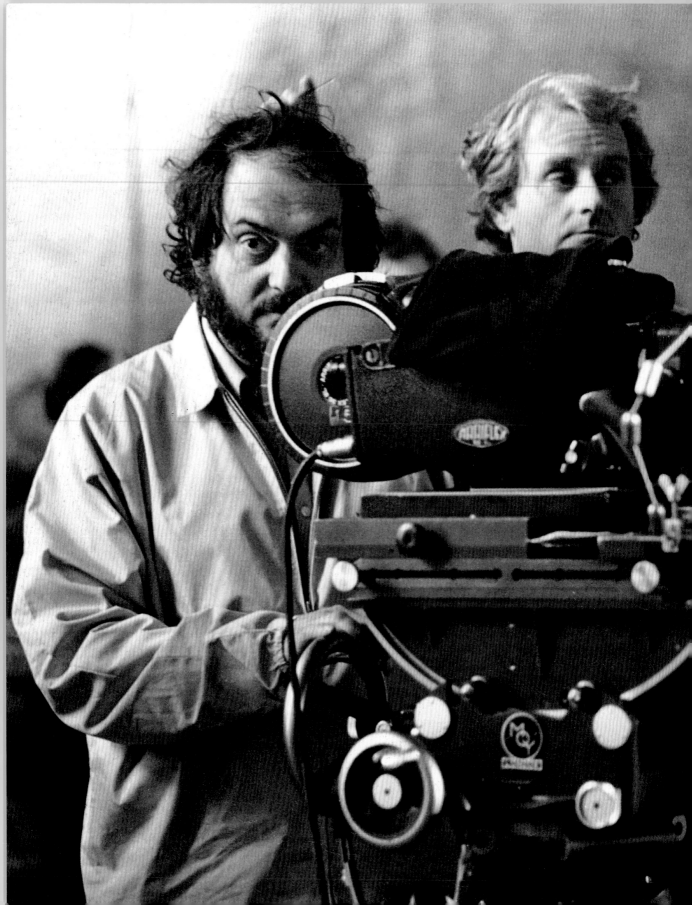

Film and painting

A powerful myth has grown up about *Barry Lyndon* that Kubrick's shots are imitations of paintings of the period. Producer Bernard Williams actually told an audience at the Academy in 2006: 'We used to copy the paintings in terms of light and where people were sitting. If you look at the movie, every scene is like a painting.' But no scholar has come forward with a single example of literal imitation from the film.

Many of Kubrick's discussions about eighteenth-century painting were not with John Alcott, his cameraman, but with Ken Adam, his production designer, and Milena Canonero, his costume designer. He wanted to take the audience into the past, and paintings were his windows into time. The portraits by Gainsborough and Reynolds showed him how people looked, wore their clothes and confronted their world, while a Hogarth narrative like the macabre *Marriage A-la-Mode*, about a doomed marriage between a penniless lord and a merchant's daughter, contained scores of details about mores, public and private, which served as touchstones for Kubrick and his collaborators. Thackeray's novel, written almost a century after the events are supposed to have taken place, was also an archaeological dig, as we are reminded by the sudden chasm that Kubrick's epilogue announces: 'They are all one now.' Written, not spoken, the epilogue is an example of an eighteenth-century poetic genre that might be found embedded in paintings or encountered in picturesque natural settings: the inscription, which served as a *memento mori* for the traveller waylaid by its words.

Kubrick put together an archive of thousands of reproductions of paintings cut from books and used them as shorthand with his collaborators. Williams recalls: '"Stanley," I'd say, "we need a call sheet for tomorrow." So he'd say, "Get all the paintings out." The paintings became our Bible. He'd go through all the paintings and say, "Well, I might do *that* tomorrow, I might do *that* tomorrow, and I might do *that* tomorrow. Get them all ready."' However, judging from the film, once the set and the models were dressed, Kubrick and Alcott filmed real landscapes and interiors using natural light (a sound stage would have been more appropriate for literal copying) in the spirit of the later eighteenth-century painters – especially Gainsborough, who painted hundreds of landscapes and also included landscape views in the portraits he is best known for. Kubrick's motto, as I once wrote concerning *Full Metal Jacket*, could be that of the seventeenth-century haiku master Matsuo Basho: 'I do not seek to follow in the footsteps of the men of old. I seek the thing they sought.'

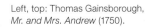

Left, top: Thomas Gainsborough, *Mr. and Mrs. Andrew* (1750).

Left, bottom: William Hogarth, *Marriage-A-la-Mode: I. The Marriage Settlement* (1743).

Above: Ryan O'Neal and Marisa Berenson in *Barry Lyndon* (1975).

the scene of the duel at the end. For inspiration Kubrick went back to the moment in *Spartacus* when Woody Strode refuses to put Douglas to death after winning their duel, choosing instead to die attacking the aristocratic spectators. In the unbearably dragged-out duel scene, Barry, who has his stepson at his mercy, fires into the ground and is repaid for it by the loss of his leg. His heroic action is a moral choice, as is Bullingdon's decision to maim the man who spared his life, acting on behalf of a whole class in ridding it of an upstart who is in the process of squandering 'a fine family fortune'.

The Shining: the five repetitions

In the aftermath of his most daring experiment, Kubrick moved to a secluded country estate in Hertfordshire, and his legend grew. After a two-year hiatus he accepted Warner Bros.' proposal to film Stephen King's *The Shining*, a story about four characters in a hotel full of ghosts. Mammoth sets were built that might have been designed by Albert Speer and Hiawatha, and much of the film was shot with a Steadicam, a new invention for moving the camera without tracks. The script by novelist Diane Johnson underwent many rewrites during

production, which took almost a year — one conversation was filmed 147 times.

Reviewers thought it ridiculous for Kubrick to foist off a roomful of cobwebby skeletons on audiences who had every right to expect groundbreaking special effects, but those skeletons aren't what is frightening in *The Shining*. The film is full of uncanny images, such as the bartender with the fixed smile whose true nature (real or imaginary, living or dead, human or machine) is impossible to determine; and the key to its style is uncanny repetition, which is no longer just a matter of enigmatic detail, or even of plot structure. The uncanniness we experience in *The Shining* is our aesthetic experience of the film itself — as a universe built out of repetitions.

Repetition 1 (Self-quotation): Studying the first kind of repetition in Kubrick's films can take us down some very strange paths. The subjective shot of the bathroom door being opened by Humbert to reveal the tub where his wife is supposedly bathing is repeated in *The Shining* when Jack Torrance opens the door of the bathroom in Room 237 of the Overlook Hotel and sees a beautiful woman in a bath, hidden behind the half-pulled shower curtain. The woman draws back the curtain, gets out of the tub, embraces him and is transformed into the rotted corpse of an old hag who was murdered (as Humbert intends to murder Charlotte) in her bath. The two images set up intriguing resonances (desiring the daughter, embracing the mother) that become downright creepy when we replay the moment in *2001* where Dave Bowman inspects the bathroom of the 'hotel room' his extra-terrestrial hosts have put him in, with György Ligeti's 'Atmospheres' babbling on the soundtrack, and fancy we hear the distorted sound of a woman crying 'Help me' just after his gaze falls on the bathtub.

Repetition 5 (Internal repetitions): According to Freud's essay 'The Uncanny', coincidental repetition — what we would call an 'uncanny coincidence' — is a potent stimulus for that weird emotion, concerning which Kubrick told Ciment: 'Freud said that the uncanny is the only feeling that is more powerfully experienced in art than in life. If the genre required any justification, I think this alone would serve as its credentials.'[23]

Freud's example of an uncanny repetition is the coincidence of multiple encounters with the

number sixty-two in a single day, suggesting perhaps that sixty-two is the age one will be when one dies. (He was sixty-two when he wrote the essay.) In *The Shining* the magic number is forty-two: it appears on the sleeve of the jersey Danny is wearing when he has his first vision of the elevator spouting blood; in a TV newscast that mentions a '$42 million budget'; in the title of the film Wendy and Danny are watching: *Summer of '42*; and hiding (like CRM-114 on the label of Alex's medicine bottle) in the name of Room 237 ($2 \times 3 \times 7 = 42$) and the caption on the photograph disclosed by the tracking shot that shows Jack surrounded by revellers at a 4th of July festivity at the Overlook in 1921 ($21 \times 2 = 42$.)

These calculations appear in a book by historian Geoffrey Cocks, arguing that Kubrick, who grew up during World War II and its aftermath, was haunted by the Shoah, but could not treat the subject directly. Instead he planted

references to 1942 — the year Himmler ordered the Final Solution put into effect at the Wannsee Conference — in *The Shining*, where Cocks believes that every enigmatic detail points to the unspoken topic: even the light-blue credits rising upwards at the beginning, accompanied by Berlioz's orchestration of the medieval *Dies Irae*, which evoke the smoke of the crematoria.

Repetition 4 (Repetition compulsion): Shelley Duvall has compared the experience of making *The Shining* to the film *Groundhog Day*, itself a brilliant exercise in uncanny repetition. Perhaps it is the weight of repetition behind each image that compels us to watch *The Shining* over and over — a quality it shares with the films of Robert Bresson, who would reportedly film a shot of a hand eighty times.

Repetition breaks through to the surface in *The Shining* in the same way it does in all Kubrick films — through botched continuity. When Jack

The Shining: Room 237

Danny has ignored the order of Mr Hallorann ('Scatman' Crothers), the chef at the Overlook, by going into Room 237. ('Mom?', he says as he pushes open the door.) He returns traumatized by what he saw. Wendy tells Jack that there is a crazy woman in Room 237 who tried to strangle their son, and he goes to investigate.

The sequence that follows takes an oblique approach to showing the first two dangerous encounters with the dead in King's story. Using the fiction of 'shining' or telepathy to justify interweaving three points of view, the sequence treats shots like shifters in language ('he', 'we'), which change their meaning depending on who is uttering them.

Hallorann is enjoying his winter vacation in Florida when his gift of 'shining' tells him that something terrible is happening at the hotel. The camera dollies in on him as the vision grows in his mind. (This shot reportedly took more than a hundred takes to film.) Cut to the point of view of someone – only if this is a flashback can it be Danny, who is shown drooling and traumatized in his bed – pushing open the door to Room 237 and entering.

Note the twin lamps framing the couch and bed, like the twin lamps framing the TV and bed in Hallorann's bedroom.

A Steadicam shot, accompanied by a heartbeat on the soundtrack, takes us to the door of the bathroom, which is pushed open, and we see that there is someone in the bathtub, hidden behind the shower curtain. (Figures seen at a distance are almost always frightening in Kubrick's films. We don't know what they might turn out to be when they come close to us.) Now a reverse shot shows us that we are seeing the scene from the point of view of Jack, who has come to investigate. He is delighted to discover that the bather is a beautiful girl.

But when he embraces her, he realizes by looking in the mirror that she has turned into a rotting corpse. The shot where he looks in the mirror, with only one eye visible, recalls the shot of Humbert looking at Lolita's photograph while attempting to make love to her mother. Within the context of the total Kubrick text, made up of all the films, is this scene Mother's revenge? Three cutaways to Danny are intercut with shots that show us what he saw in Room 237 – the corpse rising, as if levitating, from the bathtub – while the continued intercutting of Jack and the corpse as it walks towards him, laughing with outstretched arms, also shows us what Danny saw after it got out of the tub.

Unlike Danny, who was physically attacked, Jack escapes unharmed, locks the door behind him and flees – not like a man in terror, but like a man running away from something he has locked away because he wants to keep it a secret. (In the next scene he calmly tells Wendy that he found 'nothing at all' in Room 237.) Horror is still visible on his face, but his body language is almost furtive. This moment, filmed with Jack Nicholson silhouetted in a darkened hallway, is the kind of thing that must have required many takes to discover. 'The way Stanley makes a movie is the way movies should be made', Nicholson told the press. 'Everybody else is just cutting corners.'

Opposite page: Jack Nicholson in *The Shining* (1980).

Right: Scatman Crothers, Danny Lloyd and Jack Nicholson in *The Shining* (1980).

Following pages: Jack Nicholson and Joe Turkel in *The Shining* (1980).

uses an axe to smash a hole in the bathroom door behind which Wendy is cowering, the shape of the hole is different each time we see it because the director has put the sequence together from many repetitions of one action. Thematically, repetition seeps through as the idea of timelessness, beginning with the disconcerting temporal indication 'Tuesday'— Tuesday of which week? When was Monday? — and ending with the photo of Jack Torrance at the Overlook Hotel on the 4th of July, 1921. When the caretaker's ghost tells Jack 'You have always been the caretaker', the dreamlike assertion is redolent of the timelessness Freud attributed to the contents of the Unconscious.

Repetition 3 (Adaptation): Alex Cox's lapidary formula, 'no influence but himself', is really a way of saying that Kubrick valued originality, a point Alexander Walker makes by referring to Cocteau's 'Astonish us'. In fact, Kubrick rarely talked that way. More typical of his irony is something Jack Nicholson recalls in the Harlan documentary: 'Every scene has already been done', the director told him while they were filming *The Shining*. 'Our job is just to do it a little better.'[24] Or Kubrick's assertion in *Sight & Sound* that in doing an adaptation, it is the filmmaker's duty 'to be one hundred per cent faithful to the author's meaning'. These statements, paradoxically, go to the heart of Kubrick's achievement, which was to invent a new style for each film — one that was also, each time, a whole new world. But he was a modest demiurge, conscious of the limits of his powers.

Kubrick told Ciment[25] that he liked the way Stephen King in *The Shining* maintained the ambiguity of Jack Torrance's perceptions, only to reveal at a crucial point that the ghosts are real. So why does he show us the ghosts through Danny's eyes even before the family gets to the hotel? Once Danny has seen the ghostly sisters and the elevator disgorging its cargo of blood, the spectator has no reason to doubt that the Overlook is haunted. Instead, the growing horror in the film is the realization that the ghosts are trying to make Jack, a recovering alcoholic with violent tendencies, murder his wife and child, who are snowed in with no way of escaping. The danger at the Overlook is not those silly skeletons — it's something that could be happening in the house or the apartment next door to us, an interpretation King objected to even though it is what makes this particular ghost story so frightening.

Repetition 2 (Transumption): In the panoply of repetitions, the main event is the one that pits the filmmaker against his predecessors, whose potent example could paralyse his gifts. That is the subject of *The Shining*, where 'All work and no play makes Jack a dull boy' expresses Jack's fear that giving up alcohol has made him creatively (and perhaps sexually) impotent.

Harold Bloom follows Freud in interpreting the Uncanny as the sensation produced in the mind by 'something repressed which recurs', but differs from him by locating the source of the sensation, in literature, in anxiety about the return of an artistic precursor who has been repressed. Kubrick adopted Freud's own version of the theory, which traces the Uncanny to anxiety provoked by the return of repressed thoughts about more universal matters such as sex and death, when he was making *The Shining*, but the poet in him turned King's ghost story into a fable about the anxiety of influence.

This time the ancestor Kubrick was measuring himself against is the author of *Psycho*. Jack is the successor to Delbert Grady, the suavely British caretaker who chopped up his family back in the 1970s. If Jack repeats Grady's sacrifice, the ghost promises him, he can ingratiate himself with the hotel's spectral clientele and take his place. Instead, through the temporal paradox of transumption, Jack becomes one of the people in the Gold Room on the 4th of July, 1921 — the central figure in the photograph, perhaps even the host of the endless party it portrays. The Star Child and Jack's frozen image in the photograph are two sides of the same ambivalent idea: Gnostic immortality achieved at the cost of all that we value as our humanity.

The film-brain

For Kubrick's fans, the waits between films were getting longer. *Full Metal Jacket*, an adaptation of *The Short-Timers*, Gustav Hasford's nightmare novel about the Vietnam War,[26] appeared seven years after *The Shining*. The cast was led by Matthew Modine, Vincent D'Onofrio and R. Lee Ermey, whose pop-eyed, screaming performance as a Marine Corps drill instructor (which he had been in real life) dominates the first half.

Signs in Vietnamese, wrecking balls, palm trees, burning oil and burning tyres turned an

Opposite page: Scatman Crothers in *The Shining* (1980).

Below: Vincent D'Onofrio in *Full Metal Jacket* (1987).

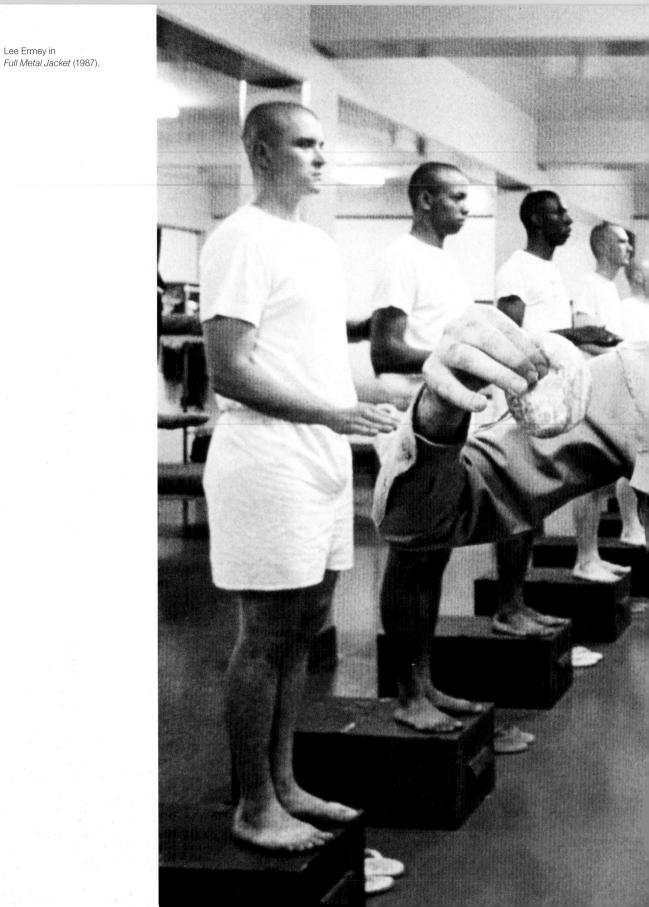

Lee Ermey in
Full Metal Jacket (1987).

abandoned gasworks into the city of Hue for the film's nerve-wracking climax. Filmed at twilight, the colours in these scenes are as gorgeous as a Rothko canvas. The international box office more than justified the film's production schedule, which included nine months of actual shooting plus a number of weeks for reflection and discussion. This ascetic approach enabled the filmmaker to scrape away every trace of anti-war rhetoric and make a film that simply showed war 'as a phenomenon'.

In the first half of *Full Metal Jacket*, set on Parris Island, the camera follows the constant parading of the recruits and their instructor, and movement is almost exclusively from the interior of the screen outwards; in the second half, set in Vietnam, movements into the image, towards the vanishing point, predominate. But the film's two parts describe a single movement with a single end-point — the encounter with a fellow human being whose face has become a 'war face', the face of death.[27]

The master of ceremonies in *Full Metal Jacket* is modelled on the character played by Peter Ustinov in *Lola Montès*. In the first scene of that film, the camera tracks backwards as the ringmaster walks towards us, spieling to the audience, between two rows of uniformed pages, and Sergeant Hartman makes his entrance the same way, walking past a column of men at attention while he announces at the top of his lungs what they are in for under his tutelage. The killing machine Hartman constructs on Parris Island eventually malfunctions when he encounters Pyle in the latrine wearing his 'war face', shown in close-up as madness, and dies.

Kubrick told *Newsweek* that in *Full Metal Jacket* he wanted to 'explode the narrative structure of film', and the first casualty of the explosion is the conventional notion of character. *Full Metal Jacket* is a film without a hero. Its only protagonist is the group mind whose formation is shown in the scenes on Parris Island, most of which portray the process of indoctrination with little reference to combat training *per se*. The death of Hartman, the master of ceremonies, signals the beginning of the film's second half, in which we follow scattered pieces of the group mind as they are set adrift in a world where scene follows scene with no apparent dramatic necessity.

In the second section of *Full Metal Jacket* we meet a whole new cast of highly individualistic

Above, top: Matthew Modine, Dorian Harewood and Adam Baldwin in *Full Metal Jacket* (1987).

Above, bottom: John Stafford in *Full Metal Jacket* (1987).

Opposite page: Ngoc Le in *Full Metal Jacket* (1987).

Following pages: Adam Baldwin and Matthew Modine in *Full Metal Jacket* (1987).

'A bedroom that's too big', by Michel Chion

In the end we have to return to childhood, the place where *2001* ends, but also to the self-confidence with which, when it deals with human history, it shows us a man asleep – Floyd. Just as the *Discovery* is too big for Floyd when he sleeps alone and is its only passenger; in the same way, at the end, Dave's bedroom and his bed are too big just for him. The term 'astral foetus' – the title of an essay by Jean-Paul Dumont and Jean Monod – is apt, but we should not forget that the idea of a foetus presupposes (symbolically at least) that it has a placenta and is contained inside a mother's womb. The presence of this giant foetus 'mammarizes' the universe (to borrow Françoise Dolto's expression), associating it with maternal security and making interplanetary space no longer hostile but protective. The spirit of childhood has long been part of Kubrick's world: Lolita's childish laughter (which is not reduced to a facet of her role

as a sex-object), Ryan O'Neal's poorly defined, 'unfinished' face in *Barry Lyndon*, and George C. Scott's childlike quality in *Dr. Strangelove*, with his nervous habit of chewing peanuts, are a few examples.

Kubrick often introduces only children, who are a bit lonely: Heywood has just one small daughter, whom he affectionately calls 'Squirt' and who seems to be spoiled; Lolita is an only daughter; Alex in *A Clockwork Orange* an only son, like little Danny in *The Shining*; Helena, in *Eyes Wide Shut*, is (for the moment?) an only daughter. Redmond Barry, in *Barry Lyndon*, has no brothers or sisters, and has only one child of his own, a boy, whom he loses. This makes the mother–son relationship both intimate and touching: Lady Lyndon and her son, in *Barry Lyndon*; Wendy and Danny in the maze, in *The Shining*. In Kubrick's hands, the relationship between HAL and the monolith is not so very far from being

like that of a Mummy and Daddy with their child. Like Alex in *A Clockwork Orange*, who is asocial and ultra-violent but drinks milk and lives with his parents, the bedroom in which Dave is 'lodged' at the end of the film has a 'mothering' ambience, echoing the one that reassures HAL. As we have seen, food, in its basic sense, plays an important role in many of Kubrick's films. We need only look at the emphasis in *The Shining* on the abundance of food stores, and the depiction of the Overlook Hotel as an enormous larder, or the comic scene in *Dr. Strangelove* involving Major Kong's survival kit, and the custard-pie fight, which was removed from the final cut. Nor should we forget the opening shot in *A Clockwork Orange*, with Alex drinking his 'Milk Plus', nor the first time we see Danny in *The Shining*, eating bread and butter, or the fact that the first part of *Full Metal Jacket* is built around the bulimia of one of the marines. Lastly, the scene

of Poole's birthday hinges on a virtual cake, transmitted as an image, which his parents show him, but which Poole will be unable to eat. The scene is not pathetic, only touching. The parents' simplicity is genuine and sincere – it's the context that makes them 'little, very little parents', around the image of a cake. But you can't eat an image. That reminds us that *2001* was inspired by the *Odyssey*, and that epic has a closer relationship with food than one might have suspected.

This is an extract from *Stanley Kubrick, l'humain, ni plus ni moins*, Cahiers du cinéma, Paris, 2006.

---

characters who are imbued with the full range of human emotions. Cut loose from their narrative moorings, they appear as opaque fragments of the larger whole, their acts legible only as 'behaviours', to borrow a term from the science of operant conditioning, in which are imbedded with a kind of horrible monotony the traits — racism, misogyny, machismo, homicidal mania — that govern the group mind, even in its malfunctioning.

Then a new antagonist erupts in the encounter with the sniper in Hue, permitting the filmmaker to start turning the screws of suspense in time to arrest the fatal drift, until the spell is shattered when he cuts to a medium close-up of the wounded teenage sniper's face as she begs Joker to kill her. Her death sets the hero adrift again. The last shots of the film showing him marching with the marauding hoard, singing the Mickey Mouse Club Song, recall the Dionysian mobs at the beginning of 'Le Masque' and the end of 'La Maison Tellier' in *Le Plaisir*: images of a world without a master of ceremonies.

Below: Stanley Kubrick with Marie Richardson on the set of *Eyes Wide Shut* (1999).

Opposite page: Stanley Kubrick with Tom Cruise and Nicole Kidman on the set of *Eyes Wide Shut* (1999).

Postscript

Warner Bros. would have been happy to make any of Kubrick's subsequent projects: Patrick Süskind's *Perfume*; *Wartime Lies*, Louis Begley's novel about the Shoah, to star Julia Roberts; or *A.I.*, which he spent 15 years developing from a Brian Aldiss story about an android boy. Because computer technology hadn't reached the point that would permit him to make the latter, *A.I.* (2001) was to be filmed after his death by Steven Spielberg. Instead, Kubrick revived an even older project.

His last film broke all records for length of time between films, length of conception (Kubrick and Warner Bros. had first announced a film based on Arthur Schnitzler's *Traumnovelle* during post-production on *A Clockwork Orange*) and production schedule: the story about a married couple succumbing to 'the seven-year itch', starring married actors Tom Cruise and Nicole Kidman, took 400 days to shoot. Like one of the film's minor characters whom we never see, Kubrick died peacefully in his sleep on 7 March 1999, a week after screening the finished film for Cruise, Kidman and Warner

Bros.. Expecting a pornographic extravaganza, critics scratched their heads, but *Eyes Wide Shut* (1999) has been winning adherents ever since, one spectator at a time, like all of Kubrick's late films. Perhaps in time we will all come around to his opinion, which was that his last film was his best. For the moment it is a bit early to say too much about *Eyes Wide Shut*, not much more than a decade old.

The source novel is by Schnitzler, who wrote the play that Ophuls made into *La Ronde*, but never has an Ophuls tribute been more abstract. The systems of interpretation — Freudian, Marxist, self-reflexive, Gnostic — that infiltrated critical vocabularies during the Kubrick years can be applied with only a token effort on the part of the spectator. Perhaps they are the worldview of an era that will soon be over, like the Renaissance cosmos that was represented in the structure and decorations of the theatre used by Shakespeare and his players. Having assumed its final form, this late twentieth-century cosmos can be treated as a series of clichés by the film, which has no other meanings to propose, but has mastered these. Bill Harford,

a well-to-do Manhattan physician, is essentially a water-boy for rich clients like Victor Ziegler, whose hooker for the evening, Mandy, Bill revives after she passes out from an overdose during a Christmas party. Bill's night away from home, after his wife reveals an old sexual fantasy to him, only brings him back to where he started, as Ziegler's well-paid subject. His revolt has been noticeably less successful than Alex's — he returns to the marriage he had to begin with, his place in the universe.

A virtual remake of Karl Grune's film *Die Strasse*, which was released in 1923, two years before Schnitzler wrote his novel, *Eyes Wide Shut* has the ritualistic feel of a tale that has been told many times — a feeling that is reinforced by the fake New York sets, which are re-dressed and re-used to represent different locales, just like the New York sets that once stood on the backlots of all the Hollywood studios.

Eyes Wide Shut is a faithful adaptation of a book that Kubrick, after brooding over it for a quarter of a century, filmed intact and virtually unchanged except for the transposition to New York in the 1990s. The one addition, which was proposed by screenwriter Frederic Raphael, is Ziegler, who ties together the Christmas party and the masked ball, and explains the rules of the game

Opposite page:
Nicole Kidman and Tom Cruise in
Eyes Wide Shut (1999).

Below: Nicole Kidman in
Eyes Wide Shut (1999).

Eyes Wide Shut: The Waltz

During the Christmas party at the beginning of *Eyes Wide Shut*, Alice (Nicole Kidman) is standing alone at the drinks table when a 180-degree camera move brings Sandor (Sky Dumont), the seductive Hungarian, into the frame. After he kisses her hand, a 180-degree cut begins their conversation. Dissolve to them dancing, turning constantly and exchanging screen positions every few seconds as in a classic Hollywood scene of a couple waltzing.

Whereas a director like Max Ophuls would move the camera in or out to vary the angle for filming the couple, Kubrick films their exchanges of screen position from one unvarying distance. They are presumably moving around the room in a circle, but the shallow focus makes their trajectory appear to be a straight line, so the camera appears to follow them in a lateral tracking shot, as if their verbal sparring match – slowed down by drunken pauses for reflection on Alice's part – were being diagrammed on a blackboard.

to Bill — an affable master of ceremonies whose merry-go-round isn't about to break down, unless that is what almost happens when Bill starts to kiss Mandy's dead face at the morgue (Corridor C, Room 114), where his quest for the mystery woman from the orgy comes to an end as Ziegler's phone call reels him back in.

Revisiting in the light of day the prostitute's apartment, the nightclub, the costume shop and the mansion where the orgy was held, Bill experiences uncanny repetitions of all the impulses he strangled during his night on the town. Perhaps he is even beginning to understand that he is in the hands of a cruel god who must be a lot like his jovial host, a god whose high priest is the master of ceremonies in the red robe. By the last scene, the Harfords are back in the circular trenches of consumer society.

This interpretation, which has been proposed by critics like Jean Douchet and Tim Kreider, is the antithesis of Michel Chion's reading of the film as a hopeful story about the hidden depths of daily life — a 'comedy of remarriage', in fact: the utopian genre discerned by the American philosopher Stanley Cavell in 1930s films like *The Awful Truth*. Chion's analysis is just as convincing as the cynical one I've outlined.

So let that be that as far as *Eyes Wide Shut* is concerned, for now. The film's reputation is growing, one spectator at a time, and it is already starting to be called a masterpiece. But its mystery remains.

Opposite page:
Tom Cruise and Nicole Kidman in *Eyes Wide Shut* (1999).

Above: Nicole Kidman and Sky Dumont in *Eyes Wide Shut* (1999).

Following pages:
Sydney Pollack and Tom Cruise in *Eyes Wide Shut* (1999).

Chronology

1928
26 July. Stanley Kubrick is born to Jack (Jacob) Kubrick and Gertrude Perveler, the children of Austrian (from the region of Galicia) immigrants. Kubrick's father is a homeopathic doctor. The family lives in the West Bronx, home to much of New York's Jewish middle class.

1940
Kubrick is sent to Pasadena, California, to live with his uncle Martin Perveler, a successful businessman, in the hope of improving his attitude towards school. His father teaches him to play chess.

1941
He returns to New York unrepentant. For his thirteenth birthday he receives his first still camera.

1942
Kubrick's family moves to a luxury apartment building on the Bronx's Grand Concourse, and Kubrick enrolls at Howard Taft High School. He reads a book that he happens to find in his father's waiting-room, which makes a big impression on him: Humphrey Cobb's World War I novel *Paths of Glory*.

1943–5
At Taft, Kubrick joins the school magazine as a photographer. He also becomes a jazz drummer.

Stanley Kubrick in the 1930s.

1945
April. Kubrick sells his first photo to *Look* magazine for $25 and is hired as an apprentice photographer.

1948
Kubrick marries Toba Metz, his high-school girlfriend, and moves to Greenwich Village.

1949
The 18 January issue of *Look* runs Kubrick's seven-page photo-essay on middleweight boxer Walter Cartier.

1950
With Alex Singer, Kubrick makes *Day of the Fight*, a short documentary (released in 1951) about Cartier, and sells it to RKO, which finances a second documentary on a subject the studio proposes, *Flying Padre*. **26 April.** *Day of the Fight* is screened at the Paramount Theatre with a Robert Mitchum picture, and Kubrick leaves his job at *Look*. With Taft friend Howard Sackler, he writes the script for *Fear and Desire*.

1951
Backed by his father and his uncle in California, he shoots *Fear and Desire* during the summer. To earn money for post-production, he makes *The Seafarers*, a documentary for the Seafarers International, and directs second-unit sequences for a television series about Lincoln written by James Agee. Toba Metz and Kubrick divorce.

1952
November. He sells *Fear and Desire* to leading art-house distributor Joseph Burstyn.

1953
Alex Singer introduces Kubrick to his future producing partner, James B. Harris. Kubrick begins a liaison with Ruth Sobotka, a ballerina who becomes his second wife. Kubrick and Sackler write a new script that will become *Killer's Kiss*.

Stanley Kubrick in the 1940s.

1954
With financing from a family friend, *Killer's Kiss* is shot in New York. United Artists buys the film.

1955
Harris–Kubrick Productions is formed. The new partners acquire the Lionel White novel *Clean Break* and hire Jim Thompson to write a screenplay (*The Killing*), which United Artists agrees to finance. Kubrick and Harris move to Los Angeles to make the picture.

1956
Dore Schary gives the partners a forty-week development deal at MGM. At the same time they acquire *Paths of Glory* and start developing a screenplay. United Artists again puts up the money after they get a star to sign on: Kirk Douglas, who will produce the film through his own company.

1957
Filming of *Paths of Glory* in Munich. Ending a troubled relationship, Ruth Sobotka and Kubrick divorce. Kubrick meets Christiane Harlan, who plays the captive German girl at the end of the film. Opening in the U.S. on Christmas Day, the film is banned in France until 1976.

Stanley Kubrick on the set of *Killer's Kiss* (1955).

1958
Christiane Harlan and Kubrick are married. While his new partner Kirk Douglas is shooting *The Vikings*, Kubrick develops *One-Eyed Jacks* for Marlon Brando, but parts company with the star before the start of production.

1959
Hired to replace Anthony Mann after two weeks shooting, Kubrick directs Douglas's *Spartacus* with an all-star cast. During production, he and Harris buy Vladimir Nabokov's best-seller, *Lolita*.

1960
Nabokov agrees to write the screenplay while Kubrick wraps up post-production on *Spartacus*, which becomes the top-grossing film of 1960.

1961
Lolita is filmed in England with a screenplay by Kubrick (uncredited), and financed by Seven Arts.

1962
Acquired for release by MGM in February, *Lolita* premieres at the Venice Film Festival and becomes one of the top-grossing pictures of the year. Harris and Kubrick buy Peter George's *Red Alert* for their next picture, which will be made for Columbia. During pre-production, they sever their partnership so that Harris can direct his own films. As the start of production looms, Kubrick brings in Terry Southern to turn the picture into a comedy.

Stanley Kubrick on the set of *2001: A Space Odyssey* (1968).

1963

April. *Dr. Strangelove* wraps after fifteen weeks of shooting in England. During filming, Peter Sellers gives Kubrick a copy of Anthony Burgess's *A Clockwork Orange*.

1964

January. *Dr. Strangelove* opens in the U.S. and does very good business. Kubrick buys a home in England and moves there permanently with his growing family. **17 May.** Kubrick hires Arthur C. Clarke to write a film about the human race's first contact with extra-terrestrials.

1965

February. MGM announces the new project.

1966

May. Finished with the actors, Kubrick begins the period of effects work and post-production.

1968

April. *2001: A Space Odyssey* opens in one theatre in New York and, after a shaky start, becomes an enormous hit. With financing from MGM, Kubrick begins research for his planned epic, *Napoleon*.

1969

Kubrick puts *Napoleon* on hold because of a change of management at MGM.

Christiane and Stanley Kubrick on the set of *Barry Lyndon* (1975).

1970

February. Warner Bros. announces a three-picture deal with Kubrick, the first picture of which will be *A Clockwork Orange*.

1971

April. During post-production on *A Clockwork Orange*, Warner Bros. announces that Kubrick's next film will be Arthur Schnitzler's *Traumnovelle (Dream Story)*. *A Clockwork Orange* opens in New York just before Christmas and becomes an international hit.

1972

Warner Bros. agrees to finance Kubrick's substitute for *Napoleon*, an adaptation of William Makepeace Thackeray's *The Memoirs of Barry Lyndon*.

1973–4

Beginning in Ireland in the autumn of 1973, principal photography for *Barry Lyndon* takes 300 days, with a ten-week hiatus when the production is moved to England after threats from the IRA. 1973 also marks the beginning of an on-off collaboration with Brian Aldiss on a film of his short story 'Supertoys Last All Summer Long'.

1974

Kubrick sees a demo reel of a new invention, the Steadicam.

1975

Released at the end of 1975, *Barry Lyndon* is drubbed by critics and ignored by audiences everywhere but in France.

1977

The Kubrick family moves into a country estate in Hertfordshire. Kubrick accepts Warner Bros.' proposal that he film Stephen King's *The Shining*.

1978

March. After the year-long filming of *The Shining* gets underway, Kubrick meets an earnest fan, Steven Spielberg.

1979

The set for the film burns. With only a few close-ups left to shoot, Kubrick insists on having it rebuilt. Shooting wraps in April.

1980

Kubrick meets Michael Herr at a preview of *The Shining*. The film opens in the U.S. in May, returning Kubrick to the Top Ten box-office list by the end of the year, despite mixed reviews.

1981

Kubrick develops, then abandons, Patrick Süskind's *Perfume*.

1982

Kubrick hires Herr to write the script of Gustav Hasford's Vietnam War novel, *The Short-Timers*.

1984

January. Warner Bros. announces plans to make Hasford's story under its new title, *Full Metal Jacket*.

1985

Kubrick's mother and father die.

1985–7

Production on *Full Metal Jacket* begins at the end of August 1985. It will not be ready for release until the summer of 1987.

1990

Kubrick restarts the development of the Aldiss story, now called *A.I.*

Stanley Kubrick on the set of *Full Metal Jacket* (1987) with his nephew Manuel Harlan.

1993

April. Warner Bros. announces that Kubrick's next film will be an adaptation of Louis Begley's story of a Jewish child escaping the Shoah by masquerading as an Aryan, *Wartime Lies*, to be re-titled *Aryan Papers*.

1995

Aryan Papers is abandoned before the start of production. In December, Warner Bros. announces a new project based on Schnitzler's *Dream Story*, starring Nicole Kidman and Tom Cruise.

1996–7

Principal photography of the new film, *Eyes Wide Shut*, takes 400 days. In March, Kubrick receives the Directors Guild of America's D. W. Griffith Award and accepts on video.

1999

7 March. After completing post-production on *Eyes Wide Shut*, Kubrick dies in his sleep, aged seventy.

2000

Steven Spielberg films *A.I.*, as he had agreed to do before Kubrick's death.

2001

A.I. is released in conjunction with Jan Harlan's *Stanley Kubrick: A Life in Pictures*.

Stanley Kubrick with Tom Cruise (top) and Sydney Pollack (bottom) on the set of *Eyes Wide Shut* (1999).

Filmography

SHORT FILMS

Day of the Fight   1951
B&W. **Format** 35mm. **Running time** 16min. With Walter Cartier.
• Before a big fight, Walter Cartier, a middleweight boxer with a promising future, goes through his pre-match preparations with his twin brother and manager, Vince. He wins – it's all in a day's work in this strange job of his.

Flying Padre   1951
B&W. **Format** 35mm. **Running time** 8min30. With Father Fred Stadtmueller, Bob Hite.
• In the New Mexico desert, Father Fred Stadtmueller visits his scattered parishioners on board a small plane that he flies himself. At the end of this short film, he picks up a sick child who needs treatment at the nearest emergency room.

The Seafarers   1953
B&W. **Format** 35mm. **Running time** 30min. With Don Hollenbeck.
• A documentary about the benefits offered to its members by the seamen's trade union. The film focuses on the union's headquarters in an unnamed city, a home away from home for seamen newly arrived in port.

FEATURE FILMS

Fear and Desire   1953
B&W. **Screenplay** Stanley Kubrick and Howard O. Sackler. **Cinematography and Editing** Stanley Kubrick. **Original Music** Gerald Fried. **Production Design** Herbert Lebowitz. **Distribution** Joseph Burstyn. **Running time** 68min. With Frank Silvera (Sgt. Mac), Kenneth Harp (Lt. Corby/enemy general), Virginia Leith (Young Girl), Paul Mazursky (Pvt. Sidney), Steve Coit (Pvt. Fletcher/enemy aide-de-camp).
• After crashing behind enemy lines, a squad of four men struggle to survive and get back to safety. One of them ends up going insane, and another dies while creating a diversion so that his comrades can kill a general and his aide-de-camp, who turn out to be older versions of themselves.

Killer's Kiss   1955
B&W. **Screenplay** Stanley Kubrick and Howard O. Sackler. **Cinematography and Editing** Stanley Kubrick. **Original Music** Gerald Fried. **Choreography** David Vaughan. **Executive Producers** Stanley Kubrick, Morris Bousel. **Production Company** Minotaur. **Distribution** United Artists. **Running time** 1h07. With Frank Silvera (Vincent Rapallo), Jamie Smith (Davy Gordon), Irene Kane (Gloria Price), Jerry Jarrett (Albert), Ruth Sobotka (Ballerina/Iris), Mike Dana, Felice Orlandi, Ralph Roberts, Phil Stevenson (Gangsters).
• Davy Gordon, a boxer preparing for his big fight, watches his neighbour in the building opposite, the beautiful Gloria, a dancer at a nightclub. He loses while Rapallo, Gloria's boss, watches on television and assaults Gloria in his excitement at seeing Davy beaten. Davy stops Rapallo from assaulting Gloria in her apartment, and they become lovers. They plan to leave together, but Rapallo has his henchmen kidnap her. Davy finds her in a loft full of store dummies and overcomes Rapallo and his thugs. The next day she shows up at the bus station where he's waiting, and the two leave town in search of a better life.

The Killing   1956
B&W. **Screenplay** Stanley Kubrick and Jim Thompson, based on the novel *Clean Break* by Lionel White. **Cinematography** Lucien Ballard. **Editing** Betty Steinberg. **Art Director** Ruth Sobotka. **Original Music** Gerald Fried. **Sound** Earl Snyder. **Executive Producer** James B. Harris. **Production Company** Harris–Kubrick Productions. **Distribution** United Artists. **Running time** 1h23. With Sterling Hayden (Johnny Clay), Jay C. Flippen (Marvin Unger), Marie Windsor (Sherry Peatty), Elisha Cook, Jr (George Peatty), Coleen Gray (Fay), Vince Edwards (Val Cannon), Ted de Corsia (Randy Kennan), Joe Sawyer (Mike O'Reilly), Timothy Carey (Nikki Arcane), Kola Kwariani (Maurice Oboukhoff), James Edwards (Track Parking Attendant), Jay Adler (Leo), Joe Turkel (Tiny).
• During his four years in jail, Johnny Clay has been planning the perfect crime: a robbery at a racetrack, which he will carry out with a group of accomplices who have no criminal records. But it all goes wrong when the inside man, George, a timid cashier at the track, tells his greedy wife, Sherry, about the plan, and she tells her lover, Val. When Val and his accomplice try to rob the robbers, everyone is killed in the shoot-out except Johnny, who is arrested at the airport while trying to get away with the loot.

Paths of Glory   1957
B&W. **Screenplay** Stanley Kubrick, Calder Willingham, Jim Thompson, based on the novel by Humphrey Cobb. **Cinematography** George Krause. **Editing** Eva Kroll. **Art Director** Ludwig Reiber. **Original Music** Gerald Fried. **Sound** Martin Müller. **Executive Producer** James B. Harris. **Production Company** Harris–Kubrick Productions. **Distribution** United Artists. **Running time** 1h26. With Kirk Douglas (Col. Dax), Ralph Meeker (Cpl. Paris), Adolphe Menjou (Gen. Broulard), George Macready (Gen. Mireau), Wayne Morris (Lt. Roget), Richard Anderson (Maj. Saint-Auban), Joseph Turkel (Pvt. Arnaud), Timothy Carey (Pvt. Ferol), Peter Capell (Judge of court-martial).
• It's World War I. General Mireau is informed by his superior officer, General Broulard, that he has to take a German position called the 'Anthill'. He agrees to do so, despite objections from Colonel Dax. The attack fails. Mireau orders his commanding officers to choose three of their men to be executed for cowardice. Dax futilely defends them at a rigged court-martial, and they are executed by a firing squad. But Dax does succeed in discrediting Mireau for having ordered a gunner to fire on his own men during the battle.

Spartacus   1960
Screenplay Dalton Trumbo, based on the novel by Howard Fast. **Cinematography** Russell Metty. **Editing** Robert Lawrence, Robert Schulte, Fred Chulack. **Production Design** Alexander Golizten. **Art Director** Eric Orbom. **Original Music** Alex North. **Sound** Waldon O. Watson, Joe Lapis, Murray Spivack, Ronald Pierce. **Producer** Edward Lewis. **Executive Producer** Kirk Douglas. **Production Company** Byna Productions Inc. **Distribution** Universal International. **Running time** International version 3h04; 1992 version 3h16. With Kirk Douglas (Spartacus), Laurence Olivier (Marcus Licinius Crassus), Jean Simmons (Varinia), Charles Laughton (Sempronius Gracchus), Peter Ustinov (Lentulus Batiatus), John Gavin (Julius Caesar), Tony Curtis (Antoninus), Nina Foch (Helena Glabrus), Herbert Lom (Tigranes Levantus), John Ireland (Crixus), John Dall (Marcius Publius Glabrus), Charles McGraw (Marcellus), Joanna Barnes (Claudia Marius), Harold J. Stone (David), Woody Strode (Draba), Peter Brocco (Ramon), Paul Lambert (Gannicus).
• Spartacus, a Thracian slave, is bought by a gladiator school, where he is trained to fight other slaves. A mutiny breaks out in the kitchens and Spartacus finds himself the head of a rebel army of former slaves, which crushes the Roman Army when it's sent against them. He marries Varinia, a slave with whom he is in love and

with whom he has a child. Spartacus pays Cicilian pirates to transport him and his army out Italy, but the reactionary senator Marcus Licinius Crassus needs the threat of a rebellion in order to abolish the constitution, and he prevents the slaves from leaving. They are defeated in their final battle and crucified, but before he dies, Spartacus sees Varinia and their child, who are now free citizens.

Lolita 1962
B&W. **Screenplay** Vladimir Nabokov, based on his novel. **Cinematography** Oswald Morris. **Editing** Anthony Harvey. **Art Director** Bill Andrews. **Original Music** Nelson Riddle (theme tune: Bob Harris). **Sound** H. L. Bird, Len Shilton. **Producer** James B. Harris. **Production Company** Seven Arts, Anya, Transworld. **Distribution** Metro-Goldwyn-Mayer. **Running time** 2h32. With James Mason (Prof. Humbert Humbert), Sue Lyon (Dolores 'Lolita' Haze), Shelley Winters (Charlotte Haze), Peter Sellers (Clare Quilty), Diana Decker (Jean Farlow), Jerry Stovin (John Farlow), Susanne Gibbs (Mona Farlow), Gary Cockrell (Richard T. Schiller, Lolita's husband), Marianne Stone (Vivian Darkbloom), Cec Linder (Dr Keegee).
• Humbert Humbert, a literature professor, rents a room from Charlotte Haze, a sexually frustrated widow with cultural pretensions, for the sole purpose of being near Lolita, her teenage daughter. When Charlotte discovers they have been flirting, she runs away and is killed in an accident. Humbert, who is now Lolita's guardian, consummates their relationship in a hotel where Clare Quilty, a famous dramatist who is also interested in Humbert's nymphette, is staying. Quilty eventually casts his spell over Lolita and steals her from Humbert. Some years later, Humbert sees her again, learns the truth and kills Quilty.

Dr. Strangelove or: 1964 How I Learned to Stop Worrying and Love the Bomb
B&W. **Screenplay** Stanley Kubrick, Terry Southern, Peter George, based on the novel *Red Alert (or Two Hours to Doom)* by Peter George. **Cinematography** Gilbert Taylor. **Editing** Anthony Harvey. **Production Design** Ken Adam. **Art Director** Peter Murton. **Special Effects** Wally Veevers. **Original Music** Laurie Johnson. **Sound** John Cox. **Producer** Stanley Kubrick. **Associate Producer** Victor Lyndon. **Production Company** Hawk Films Ltd. **Distribution** Columbia Pictures. **Running time** 1h33. With Peter Sellers (Group Captain Lionel Mandrake/President Merkin Muffley/Dr. Strangelove), George C. Scott (General 'Buck' Turgidson), Sterling Hayden (General Jack D. Ripper), Keenan Wynn (Colonel 'Bat' Guano), Slim Pickens (Major T. J. 'King' Kong), Peter Bull (Russian Ambassador Alexi de Sadesky), Tracy Reed (Miss Scott), James Earl Jones (Lieutenant Lothar Zogg), Jack Creley (Mr. Staines), Frank Berry (Lieutenant H. R. Dietrich), Glen Beck (Lieutenant W. D. Kivel).
• General Jack D. Ripper, commander of a squadron of B-52 bombers carrying atomic weapons, goes insane and orders his planes to attack Russia. The planes can be stopped only by an 'abort code' locked in Ripper's brain, so when it looks like he'll be captured, Ripper commits suicide before anyone can force him to reveal it. President Muffley contacts the Russian prime minister, Kissoff, in an attempt to avoid a catastrophe that could, if one of the bombs reached its target, set off the Doomsday Device, the Russian weapon of retaliation installed in the arctic tundra. But a bomb explodes thanks to the heroism of one of the bombardiers, and the Apocalypse is under way.

2001: A Space 1968 Odyssey
Screenplay Arthur C. Clarke and Stanley Kubrick, based on the short story 'The Sentinel' by Arthur C. Clarke. **Cinematography** Geoffrey Unsworth, Kelvin Pike. **Editing** Ray Lovejoy. **Production Design** Tony Masters, Harry Lange, Ernest Archer, Robert Cartwright, John Graysmark. **Art Director** John Hoesli. **Special Photographic Effects** directed by Stanley Kubrick. **Costumes** Hardy Amies. **Make-up** Stuart Freeborn. **Sound** Winston Ryder. **Producer** Stanley Kubrick. **Production Company** MGM. **Distribution** MGM. **Running time** 2h21. With Keir Dullea (Dave Bowman), Gary Lockwood (Frank Poole), William Sylvester (Heywood R. Floyd), Douglas Rain (HAL), Daniel Richter (Moon-Watcher), Leonard Rossiter (Andrei Smyslov), Margaret Tyzack (Elena).
• The dawn of humanity: a mysterious black monolith appears and brings about the sudden evolution of man's simian ancestors. 2001: another monolith, buried for millions of years near the surface of the Moon, is excavated and begins to emit a signal in the direction of Jupiter. Months later, the space ship *Discovery* is on course towards Jupiter. The super-computer HAL breaks down, causing the death of all members of the crew except one, Dave Bowman, who finds a third monolith in orbit around Jupiter. The monolith opens the Stargate, and Bowman is taken through it, embarking on an incredible journey, before being reborn as a 'Star Child', the next stage of human evolution.

A Clockwork Orange 1971
Screenplay Stanley Kubrick, based on the novel by Anthony Burgess. **Cinematography** John Alcott. **Editing** Bill Butler. **Production Design** John Barry. **Art Directors** Russell Hagg, Peter Shields. **Original Music** Walter Carlos. **Sound** Brian Blamey. **Executive Producers** Max L. Raab, Si Litvinoff. **Associate Producer** Bernard Williams. **Producer** Stanley Kubrick. **Production Company** Warner Bros., Hawk Films. **Distribution** Warner Bros. **Running time** 2h17. With Malcolm McDowell (Alexandre de Large), Patrick Magee (Mr Alexander), Michael Bates (Chief Guard), Warren Clarke (Dim), John Clive (Stage Actor), Adrienne Corri (Mrs Alexander), Carl Duering (Dr Brodsky), Paul Farrell (Tramp), Clive Francis (Lodger), Michael Gover (Prison Governor), Miriam Karlin (Catlady), James Marcus (Georgie).
• London, the near future. The young thug Alex and his 'droogs' Dim, Georgie and Pete, are abroad every night in search of sex, drugs and ultra-violence, all associated in Alex's mind with Beethoven's Ninth Symphony. Betrayed by his gang after accidentally killing somebody in the course of a burglary, Alex is sent to prison, where he volunteers to take part in an experimental programme of behaviour control, the Ludovico Technique, which will train him to fear sex, violence and Beethoven. Once released, he encounters one by one all the people he has harmed, who take their revenge. But after he attempts suicide, the government is rocked by the scandal. It makes a deal with Alex and returns his brain to its original state.

Barry Lyndon 1975
Screenplay Stanley Kubrick, based on the novel *The Memoirs of Barry Lyndon* by William Makepeace Thackeray. **Cinematography** John Alcott. **Editing** Tony Lawson. **Production Design** Ken Adam. **Art Director** Roy Walker. **Costumes** Ulla-Britt Søderlund. **Original Music** Leonard Rosenman. **Producer** Stanley Kubrick. **Executive Producer** Jan Harlan. **Associate Producer** Bernard Williams. **Production Company** Warner Bros., Hawk, Peregrine Films. **Distribution** Warner Bros. **Running time** 3h27. With Ryan O'Neal (Barry Lyndon), Marisa Berenson (Honoria Lyndon), Patrick Magee (Chevalier de Balibari), Hardy Krüger (Captain Potzdorf), Stephen Berkoff (Lord Ludd), Gay Hamilton (Nora Brady), Marie Kean (Mrs Barry, Barry Lyndon's Mother), Diana Koerner (Lischen), Murray Melvin (Reverend Samuel Runt), Frank Middlemass (Lord Lyndon), André Morell (Lord Wendover), Arthur O'Sullivan (Captain Feeny, the Highwayman), Godfrey Quigley (Captain Grogan), Leonard Rossiter (Captain Quin), Philip Stone (Graham), Leon Vitali (Lord Bullingdon), Dominic Savage

(Young Bullingdon), David Morley (Bryan, Barry Lyndon's son).

• Redmond Barry, a son of the impoverished Irish gentry, has to flee the family estate after killing – or so it seems – a British officer in the course of a duel. After a series of picaresque adventures, which include periods in the British and Prussian armies, he enters the service of a professional gambler, the Chevalier de Balibari. Redmond sets his heart on Lady Lyndon, the wife of an aged aristocrat who dies shortly afterwards. They marry, and he becomes Barry Lyndon. But he is cruelly indifferent towards his wife and stepson, Lord Bullingdon, who grows up to hate him and finally challenges him to a duel. When Bullingdon's pistol goes off accidentally, Barry gracefully fires into the ground, and Bullingdon shoots him in the leg. His leg amputated, Barry is sent back to Ireland with a pension and is barred from ever returning to England.

The Shining   **1980**
Screenplay Stanley Kubrick and Diane Johnson, based on the novel by Stephen King. **Cinematography** John Alcott. **Editing** Ray Lovejoy. **Production Design** Roy Walker. **Art Director** Les Tomkins. **Original Music** Wendy (Walter) Carlos. **Make-up** Tom Smith. **Costumes** Milena Canonero. **Sound** Ivan Sharrock. **Producer** Stanley Kubrick. **Executive Producer** Jan Harlan. **Production** Warner Bros., Hawk, Peregrine Films. **Distribution** Warner Bros. **Running time** 2h22 (US), 1h55 (EU). With Jack Nicholson (Jack Torrance), Shelley Duvall (Wendy Torrance), Danny Lloyd (Danny Torrance), Scatman Crothers (Dick Hallorann), Barry Nelson (Stuart Ullman), Philip Stone (Delbert Grady), Joe Turkel (Lloyd), Lia Beldam (Young Woman in Bath), Billie Gibson (Old Woman in Bath), Barry Dennen (Watson), David Baxt, Manning Redwood (Rangers), Lisa and Louise Burns (Grady Twin Daughters).

• Jack Torrance, a would-be writer, accepts a job as a hotel caretaker for the winter season. He goes to the Overlook Hotel with his wife, Wendy, and their son, Danny, who has powers of clairvoyance. The

hotel has a very bad reputation, since the previous caretaker killed his wife and their two daughters with an axe. Hallorann, the Overlook's chef, notices Danny's gift, which he calls 'shining'. When the Torrances are left there alone, the hotel's ghosts drive Jack to murder his family. Hallorann, who has heard Danny's telepathic distress call, is killed while trying to help them, but after Danny manages to confuse Jack in the hotel's hedge-maze, he and Wendy escape on Hallorann's snowplough and leave Jack to freeze to death.

Full Metal Jacket   **1987**
Screenplay Stanley Kubrick, Michael Herr, Gustav Hasford, based on the novel The Short-Timers by Gustav Hasford. **Cinematography** Douglas Milsome. **Editing** Martin Hunter. **Production Design** Anton Furst, Stephen Simmonds. **Art Directors** Rod Stratfold, Les Tomkins, Keith Pain. **Costumes** Keith Denny. **Original Music** Abigail Mead (Vivian Kubrick), Nigel Goulding. **Producer** Stanley Kubrick. **Executive Producer** Jan Harlan. **Co-producer** Philip Hobbs. **Production Company** A Natant Film. **Distribution** Warner Bros. **Running time** 1h56. With Matthew Modine (Joker), Adam Baldwin (Animal Mother), Vincent D'Onofrio (Pyle), R. Lee Ermey (Gny. Sgt. Hartman), Dorian Harewood (Eightball), Arliss Howard (Cowboy), Kevyn Major Howard (Rafterman), Ed O'Ross (Lt. Touchdown), John Terry (Lt. Lockhart), Kieron Jecchinis (Crazy Earl), Kirk Taylor (Payback), Tim Colceri (Doorgunner), John Stafford (Doc Jay), Bruce Boa (Poge Colonel), Ian Tyler (Lt. Cleves), Gary Landon Mills (Donlon), Sal Lopez (T. H. E. Rock).

• In a Marine Corps training camp on Parris Island, a squad of young recruits is bullied by Sergeant Hartman, an instructor with a grim sense of humour whose chosen victim is a vulnerable recruit named Pyle. The film's hero, Joker, witnesses Hartman's murder by Pyle. Cut to Danang, where Joker is a reporter for Stars and Stripes. He is sent into the countryside around Hue to join a combat unit, the Lusthogs. While the

Lusthogs are patrolling Hue, they are picked off one by one by an unseen sniper who, as Joker discovers when he penetrates her entrenched position, is just a teenage girl. Cut down by bullets, the sniper is dying, and Joker is the only one willing to put an end to her agony by shooting her in the head.

Eyes Wide Shut   **1999**
Screenplay Stanley Kubrick, Frederic Raphael, based on the novella Traumnovelle (Dream Story) by Arthur Schnitzler. **Cinematography** Larry Smith. **Editing** Nigel Galt. **Production Design** Les Tomkins, Roy Walker. **Costumes** Marit Allen. **Make-up** Robert McCann. **Original Music** Jocelyn Pook, performed by Electra Strings. **Sound** Edward Tise, Paul Conway. **Executive Producer** Jan Harlan. **Co-producer** Brian W. Cook. **Production Company** Pole Star, Hobby Films Ltd. **Distribution** Warner Bros. **Running time** 2h39. With Tom Cruise (Dr William 'Bill' Harford), Nicole Kidman (Alice Harford), Sydney Pollack (Victor Ziegler), Marie Richardson (Marion), Rade Sherbedgia (Milich), Todd Field (Nick Nightingale), Vinessa Shaw (Domino), Sky Dumont (Sandor Szavost), Fay Masterson (Sally), Madison Eginton (Helena Harford).

• Bill Harford (a New York doctor) and his wife, Alice, are tempted to be unfaithful during a Christmas party given by Ziegler, one of Bill's wealthy patients. Later, Alice demands that Bill reveal his secret desires to her and tells him one of hers. A telephone call informs Bill that one of his aged patients has just died, and he uses it as an excuse to leave the house. A series of frustrating sexual encounters leads him to don a disguise and enter a masked orgy taking place in a large country house. Bill is unmasked but is saved by the intervention of one of the prostitutes involved in the orgy. The next day, after revisiting the scenes of his frustrating night out, he finds her dead at the morgue. Ziegler explains to Bill that all the sinister events of the orgy were only a lure designed to frighten him – the prostitute has died from an overdose. Bill goes home and, in tears, confesses everything to Alice.

Selected Bibliography

John Baxter,
Stanley Kubrick: A Biography,
Carroll & Graf Publishers,
New York, 1997.

Michel Ciment,
Kubrick: The Definitive Edition,
Faber and Faber, New York, 2001.

Arthur C. Clarke,
The Lost Worlds of 2001,
New American Library, New York, 1972.

Geoffrey Cocks,
The Wolf at the Door: Stanley Kubrick, History, and the Holocaust,
Peter Lang Publishing,
New York, 2004.

Richard Corliss,
Lolita,
BFI Film Classics, BFI Publishing,
London, 1994.

Paul Duncan,
Stanley Kubrick: Visual Poet 1928–1999,
Taschen, Cologne, 2008.

Mario Falsetto,
Stanley Kubrick, A Narrative and Stylistic Analysis,
Praeger Publishers,
Westport, CT, 2001.

Michael Herr,
Kubrick,
Grove Press, New York, 2001.

David Hughes,
The Complete Kubrick,
Virgin, London, 2000.

Vincent LoBrutto,
Stanley Kubrick: A Biography,
Donald I. Fine Books, New York, 1997.

Matthew Modine,
Full Metal Jacket Diary,
Rugged Land, New York, 2005.

Gene D. Phillips (ed.),
Stanley Kubrick Interviews,
University Press of Mississippi,
Jackson, 2001.

Leonard F. Wheat,
Kubrick's 2001: A Triple Allegory,
The Scarecrow Press,
Lanham, MD, 2000.

Notes

1. Only bad video bootlegs of *Fear and Desire* are currently available. The only 35mm print is preserved at Eastman House in New York.

2. Gilles Deleuze, *Cinema 2: The Time-Image*, tr. Hugh Tomlinson and Robert Galeta, The Athlone Press, London, 1989.

3. Kubrick's brother-in-law Jan Harlan produced all his films after *Paths of Glory*. His documentary on Kubrick is available on DVD from Warner Bros.

4. Max Ophuls, who came from the Vienna theatre, made nineteen films in Germany, but his films that are best known today were made in Hollywood (*Letter from an Unknown Woman*) and France (*La Ronde, The Earrings of Madame de …*). His last completed film, *Lola Montès*, was a major box-office disappointment.

5. William Karl Guérin, *Max Ophuls*, Cahiers du cinéma, Paris, 1998.

6. Mario Falsetto, *Stanley Kubrick, A Narrative and Stylistic Analysis*, Praeger Publishers, Westport, CT, 2001, p. 4.

7. Michel Ciment, *Kubrick: The Definitive Edition*, Faber and Faber, New York, 2001.

8. Alexander Walker, 'Interview with Stanley Kubrick', *Eye Magazine* (August 1968).

9. *Cahiers du cinéma*, 150–1 (December 1963–January 1964).

10. Welles's use of wide-angle lenses in *Citizen Kane* permitted a more inclusive view of scenes and greater depth of field. Extreme wide-angle lenses create distortions that have earned them the nickname 'fish-eye lenses'.

11. Richard Corliss, *Lolita*, BFI Film Classics, BFI Publishing, London, 1994.

12. Jean-Claude Biette, 'La barbe de Kubrick', *Trafic*, 32 (1999).

13. *Sight & Sound*, 30 (1960–1).

14. Alexander Walker, *Stanley Kubrick, Director* (revised edition), W. W. Norton, London, 2000.

15. Michel Chion, *Stanley Kubrick, l'humain, ni plus ni moins*, Cahiers du cinéma, Paris, 2006.

16. In *Citizen Kane*, the mystery of a dying tycoon's last utterance is solved when the camera discloses, in the last shot of the film, the name on his childhood sled, 'Rosebud', just before it is consigned to the flames.

17. Gnosticism is the belief that the universe was created by mistake by a secondary divinity called the Demiurge. The Demiurge blocks any attempt by man to unite the divine spark hidden inside him with the true God, who resides outside Creation. Among literary and cinematic representations of Gnostic beliefs are Franz Kafka's *The Castle* (1922) and Jean Cocteau's *Orphée* (1949). The American philosopher Harold Bloom considers Gnosticism to be the religion of poets, for whom the poetic precursor is the Demiurge and his precursor is the true God.

18. Alexander Walker, *Stanley Kubrick, Director* (revised edition), W. W. Norton, London, 2000.

19. Jean-Pierre Oudart, 'À propos d'*Orange mécanique*, Kubrick, Kramer et quelques autres', *Cahiers du cinéma*, 293 (October 1978).

20. Mario Falsetto, *Stanley Kubrick, A Narrative and Stylistic Analysis*, Praeger Publishers, Westport, CT, 2001, pp. 118–22.

21. Bertolt Brecht, 'Nouvelle technique d'art dramatique', *Écrits sur le théâtre*, L'Arche, Paris, 1972. (Author's translation.)

22. Leon Vitali, presentation of *Barry Lyndon*, Academy of Motion Picture Arts and Sciences, 21 August 2006.

23. Michel Ciment, *Kubrick: The Definitive Edition*, Faber and Faber, New York, 2001.

24. Jan Harlan, *Stanley Kubrick: A Life in Pictures*, DVD, Warner Bros., 2001.

25. Michel Ciment, *Kubrick: The Definitive Edition*, Faber and Faber, New York, 2001.

26. A war correspondent who was with the Marines in Vietnam, Gustav Hasford created most of the hilarious dialogue between the boot-camp instructor and his recruits in his first novel, *The Short-Timers*.

27. cf. 'The Temptation of Mephistopheles' in William Karl Guérin, *Max Ophuls*, Cahiers du cinéma, Paris, 1998. 'The film ends up escaping the master of ceremonies … [Ophuls] suspends the roundelay with a close-up, projecting into the heart of this universe choreographed around physical states the image of a woman's face, smooth and serious, whose dimensions trouble the carefully calibrated play of attitudes.'' (Author's translation.)

Sources

Collection Cahiers du cinéma: Inside front cover, p. 2, 4–5, 14–5, 16, 17 (top), 18, 20, 21, 22, 23, 25 (bottom), 26–7, 28, 31, 34–5, 36, 37, 40–1, 43, 46–7, 52, 53, 54–5, 56, 57, 58, 60–1, 62, 65, 66–7, 71, 72–3, 74–5, 78–9, 81, 82–3, 84, 85, 86–7, 88, 89, 90, 91, 92, 94–5, 97 (3rd and 4th col.), 98 (3rd col. top), 99 (1st col.; 2nd col. top; 3rd and 4th col.), 100 (2nd and 3rd col.), 103.

Collection Cahiers du cinéma/ D. Rabourdin: p. 6, 12, 17 (bottom), 24–5, 29, 30, 32–3, 42, 44, 45, 64, 68–9, 70, 76, 80, 98 (3rd col. bottom; 4th col.), 100 (1st col.).

Collection CAT'S: p. 10, 11, 98 (2nd col. top) Museum of the city of New York: p. 7, 8–9. Screen grabs: p. 13, 48, 50, 51, 77, 93, 99 (2nd col. bottom).

Credits

© J.-P. Charbonnier: p. 96 (4th col.).
© Columbia: p. 6.
© Columbia/Sony: p. 40–1, 42, 43, 44, 45, 46–7, 99 (2nd col. top).
© Gaumont: p. 21.
© Stanley Kubrick: p. 7, 8–9.

© National Gallery/London, UK/The Bridgeman Art Library: p. 68.
© Stanley Kubrick Productions: p. 10, 11, 96 (1st and 2nd col.), 98 (2nd col. top).
© United Artists: p. 12, 13, 14–5, 16, 17 (bottom), 18, 20, 22, 23, 24–5, 25 (bottom), 26–7, 96 (3rd col.), 98 (3rd col.), 100.
© Universal: Inside front cover, p. 17 (top), 26–7, 28, 29, 30, 31, 98 (3rd col.), 100.
© Warner: p. 2, 32–3, 34–5, 36, 37, 38, 48, 49, 50, 51, 52, 53, 54–5, 56, 57, 58, 60–1, 62, 64, 65, 66–7, 68–9, 70, 71, 72–3, 74–5, 76, 77, 78–9, 80, 81, 82–3, 84, 85, 86–7, 88, 90, 91, 92, 93, 94–5, 96 (4th col.), 97, 99 (1st col.; 2nd col. bottom; 3rd and 4th col.), 100, inside back cover.
© Warner/Manuel Harlan: p. 89, 96, 103.

All reasonable efforts have been made to trace the copyright holders of the photographs used in this book. We apologize to anyone that we were unable to reach.

Cover: Stanley Kubrick on the set of *The Shining* (1980).
Inside front cover: Stanley Kubrick with Kirk Douglas and Tony Curtis. on the set of *Spartacus* (1960).
Inside back cover: Stanley Kubrick on the set of *The Shining* (1980).
Right: Stanley Kubrick on the set of *Eyes Wide Shut* (1999).

Acknowledgements

Paul Mazursky, Bernard Williams, Joseph Kaufman, Joe Dante, Christa Fuller, Jan Harlan, Brent Kite, Peter Tonguette, Hadrian Belove, Anastasia Thomas, Saul Symonds, Michael Singer and Richard Modiano.
Thanks to Michel Chion, whose filmography extracted from the book *Stanley Kubrick, l'humain ni plus, ni moins* (Cahiers du cinéma, 2006) was the basis to this one.

Cahiers du cinéma Sarl
65, rue Montmartre
75002 Paris

www.cahiersducinema.com

Revised English edition © 2010 Cahiers du cinéma Sarl
First published in French as *Stanley Kubrick* © 2007 Cahiers du cinéma Sarl

ISBN 978 2 8664 2572 2

A CIP catalogue record of this book is available from the British Library.

Series conceived by Claudine Paquot
Designed by Werner Jeker/Les Ateliers du Nord
Printed in China